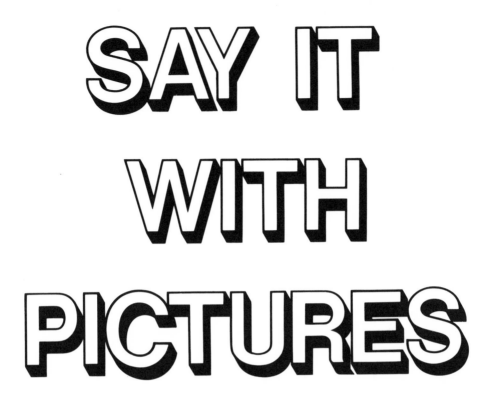

SAY IT WITH PICTURES

Graphic communication with illustration

Rod van Uchelen

VAN NOSTRAND REINHOLD COMPANY
New York   Cincinnati   Toronto   London   Melbourne

Library of Congress Catalog Card Number 78-8670

ISBN 0-442-28642-2 (cloth)
ISBN 0-442-28644-9 (Paper)

Printed in the United States of America

Published in 1979 by Van Nostrand Reinhold Company
A division of Litton Educational Publishing, Inc.
135 West 50th Street, New York, N.Y. 10020, U.S.A.

Van Nostrand Reinhold Limited
1410 Birchmount Road, Scarborough, Ontario M1P 2E7, Canada

Van Nostrand Reinhold Australia Pty. Limited
17 Queen Street, Mitcham, Victoria 3132, Australia

Van Nostrand Reinhold Company Limited
Molly Millars Lane, Wokingham, Berkshire, England

16 15 14 13 12 11 10 9 8 7 6 5 4 3 2 1

Library of Congress Cataloging in Publication Data
Van Uchelen, Rod.
  Say it with pictures.
  Includes index.
  1. Graphic arts—Technique.   I. Title.
NC730.V36   741.6   78-8670
ISBN 0-442-28642-2
ISBN 0-442-28644-9 pbk.

CONTENTS

INTRODUCTION

This is a book on illustration. It is not about how to do illustration: it is rather about how to use illustration, how to obtain illustration, and how to handle illustration. This process—concept, development, and execution—is really a design process, although it is not usually thought of as such. If one can accept that this process is design, then this is a book on graphic design.

The question of how much of an artist one must become to be an illustrator can be set aside by using the work of other more skilled artists. One is not required to become an illustrator in order to use illustration. The skill required to use illustration is no more difficult than the skill required to use the written word.

We look upon the written word as the essential element of communication, but consider that words are made up of graphic symbols. These symbols, we are told, developed from pictographs and hieroglyphs, which are also the ancestors of pictures and illustration; so perhaps words and pictures are not so different after all. Words and pictures are easily used together, but we are educated to use the former more than the latter.

There is, however, one way in which most of us are taught to use illustration, which is to make a picture for the purpose of diagramming a problem: this is the process of relating a series of steps in order to gain a clear conception of what the problem is. Many math teachers, for instance, use diagrams to clarify a written problem, and we can use pictures to clarify any written concept. This is one dictionary definition of picture, whether verbal or graphic—to make so vivid as to suggest a mental image. That illustration is so often overlooked in deference to the written word is probably due to the fact that we haven't thought about it, that we don't know how to handle the unfamiliar material.

Illustrations are pictures that are concerned with expressing an idea. Their essential purpose is communication. The way to think about the amalgam of pictures and words in the context of graphics is to think about ideas. It is as if to say, "picture this," and then, instead of giving a verbal description, to show a picture that communicates the intended idea.

An illustration is a storytelling picture. It can also decorate and illuminate, and it can do all these things separately or simultaneously. An illustration, then, can be almost any kind of picture or image whose purpose is to communicate. In the case of an illustration that is used for the purpose of decoration we may assume that it is also used to communicate the subtext—that which is implied but not stated. Art

pictures interpret and invest experience with meaning. Until we have meaning we cannot communicate, but this purpose is different from that of illustration, because illustration is less interpretive and seeks primarily to communicate. Too deep a meaning hides the communication rather than elucidating it. There is a tremendous overlap in terms of the picture itself but a strict distinction of purpose, which is clearly self-evident in how the picture is used.

Pictures communicate rapidly. Anyone can see that a picture communicates an idea more directly than do words, that a picture can communicate in its own universal language, or that a picture can communicate an abstract idea metaphorically by symbolizing the idea, with words used to cue the metaphor. Reading volumes of material can become laborious. Speed-reading courses speed up this process. If an idea can be presented in a picture supported by a few words, so much the better. After all, we watch pictures on television for relaxation.

With an education in the use of illustration we become more effective communicators. We should all be able to agree that this is useful to anyone involved in graphic communication, even if one never actually produces an illustration. This awareness is helpful to anyone who needs to assist or to hire someone else or to understand the process. The communication is the concept designed into the visual image.

Visual thinking is something that we all do habitually, but, because we take it for granted, we do not connect it with the illustration process. For example, think of yourself going home: it would be unusual if you think of words and not of the image of streets and conveyances. Thinking in images, something we normally do, helps us to find illustrations.

The creative process of finding pictures—and it is a creative process—relates simultaneously to three views of the problem of illustration: the means of achieving the objective, the availability of material, and the pragmatics of handling the material. These

I-1. This pictograph, developed from *Dancing Warriors,* a 300 B.C. cave painting but without the texture of stone and vegetable dye, is comparable to the photo of spray-painted graffiti. The symbols used are different, but the purpose is probably the same.

three points of view, although they are managed simultaneously in real life, are discussed sequentially in this book. The first question is how do you determine what you need in the way of illustration; the second, where do you get the illustration; and, finally, now that you have the illustration, how do you handle it?

This book assumes that you know how to express ideas on paper with words and that you need to do this in order to convey information—to entertain, to report, or to sell. To say it with pictures, we must also assume that there is a concept to display and, further, that there is a receptive audience, because this concept is designed for their amusement or benefit. In practical terms, if a business is involved and the purpose is to communicate a concept relating to that business, it is assumed that the originator knows the business and how to present the idea to the public and can express it in words. What we are interested in now is how to express the idea in the simplest, most interesting way—how to say it in pictures.

We are all educated to be aware of pictures. One might claim still further that in a literate, technological society we have all reached a certain level of graphic sophistication through exposure to television and advertising media. Everyone is affected by this information explosion. Much work is done at a point remote from the product, and much of what we deal with requires information. With the physical decentralization of society has arisen the need to communicate graphically. Products that we commonly use require skill to operate—it is not just a matter of flicking the ON switch—and we must understand what happens next in order to survive. That all this information be expressed graphically is necessary, but it can be enhanced and speeded up through the use of pictures. Consider the improved symbols used on international highway signs, for example. Anyone can illustrate his or her ideas; certainly we all respond to pictures. Now that illustrations are easily obtainable, they are inexpensive, even economical in terms of time, effort, and cost.

With the availability of inexpensive graphic techniques—which were once expensive—more people will use illustration. In many instances it costs no more than to use words alone. For example, if a message is to be printed using the offset-printing technique, pictures can be added at no extra expense: the graphic technique cannot distinguish between written and illustrated communication. The same is true of most copiers and of duplicators in which the printing element is made mechanically. If in some instances illustration is more expensive, it is nowhere near what it once cost. All these factors make illustration more available.

The more one advances in understanding, naturally, the better the work can be. Expertise in the subject plays a part, for graphic communication is both idea and means. Together they make up the communication. The originator may best understand the requirements of the message. This is the design, the process of concept, development, and execution, which is not much different from organizing one's thoughts to communicate in words. For example, is it enough to say that the book is on the table or is it necessary to say that the red book with leather covers is on the mahogany table? Illustrations can be extremely articulate in conveying very fine and significant detail.

The organization of illustration in most cases is best kept simple, and the imagination is best used judiciously. This book deals with the subject simply, and most of the concepts can be used by anyone, whether or not one is a trained artist. Even strictly artistic concepts can be easily understood by the nonartist. Since illustration must deal with a subject, the communication is both the concept and the means. With an understanding of your subject you need only to know the means. This book helps in this process of translating the idea into a graphic image by explaining how the artist or the designer works. Then you can say it with pictures.

Ancient Egyptian hieroglyphs look like pictures. Each picture stands for a sound. The word "merut" translates into "love." The hieroglyphs are read from the top down. The drawing of the hoe with the oval mouth below it represents "mer"; the quail chick is "u"; the loaf of bread over the chick's back is "t"; the little man at the bottom of the panel is a symbol that determines the category of human activity that the word expresses—in this case love. Considering the written word as a written pictorial symbol suggests a more direct use of pictorial symbols to illustrate an idea or concept.

USE OF ILLUSTRATION

CATEGORIES OF ILLUSTRATION BY SPECIALIZATION

PUBLICATION
- STORY ILLUSTRATION
- FIGURE ILLUSTRATION
- PRODUCT ILLUSTRATION
- EDITORIAL ILLUSTRATION
- SKETCH REPORTS
- POCKET BOOK COVERS
- BOOK ILLUSTRATION
- POLITICAL CARTOONS
- CARTOON STRIPS
- CHILDRENS BOOK ILLUSTRATION

MERCHANDISE
- WOMENS FASHION
- CHILDRENS FASHION
- MENS FASHION
- FURNITURE
- HARD LINE ITEMS

ADVERTISING
- FIGURE ILLUSTRATION
- PRODUCT ILLUSTRATION
- TECHNICAL ILLUSTRATION
- ATMOSPHERE ILLUSTRATION
- CARICATURE OR CARTOONS

TELEVISION
- REPORTORIAL SKETCHES
- BACKGROUND ILLUSTRATION
- SENIC SKETCH ILLUSTRATION
- CARTOONS & ANIMATION
- COMPUTER AIDED ILLUSTRATION

MANUFACTURING
- ARCHITECTURAL RENDERING
- PRODUCT RENDERING
- TECHNICAL ILLUSTRATION
- PACKAGING ILLUSTRATION

SPECIAL SUBJECT
- WILDLIFE ILLUSTRATION
- MEDICAL ILLUSTRATION
- SCIENTIFIC ILLUSTRATION
- WESTERN ILLUSTRATION
- INDUSTRIAL ILLUSTRATION
- SPORTS ILLUSTRATION

SPECIAL TECHNIQUES
- BLACK & WHITE ARTIST
- SCRATCHBOARD ARTIST
- AIRBRUSH ARTIST
- WATERCOLORIST

1. KINDS OF ILLUSTRATION

So many kinds of pictures are used to illustrate ideas that one should realize at the outset that there are no boundaries or limits of expression and no correct or incorrect ways in which pictures can communicate. There are, however, categories of specialization according to the market for a particular kind of illustration. Again, various materials have shaped technical conventions, and the mechanical requirements of reproduction make some methods more appropriate than others for a given use. That these diverse factors are in constant interplay should be obvious, and the field of illustration is in constant change.

Defining the concept of illustration in its largest sense—to include all the ways in which ideas are pictured—it ranges from engineering drawings that picture construction to instant photographs that picture a happy moment. This is a wider definition of the term "illustration" than that denoting a specific kind of picture, yet it conforms to the intent of illustration used to communicate an idea. This is the scope of illustration, whether technical illustration done in isometric drawings or magazine illustration using candid photos. In all cases the purpose of the picture is to present an idea or concept.

Against the wide variety of illustration the use of pictures can best be thought of in relation to the purpose to which it will be put, the need. Illustration can be categorized arbitrarily in a variety of ways, such as by schools of art or by art technique, and this is sometimes useful, but all these categories are subordinate to the practical purpose of the illustration, which is to communicate. It is more accurate therefore to view illustration as deriving from usage. The use of illustration as a medium of communication is influenced by the practical requirements of technique.

Out of this point of view the user can find the most available art and the easiest techniques, which emerge from the need. The many practical considerations of what is to be communicated, the availability of material, and the techniques used are balanced against the specifics of time, money, and effort required. The need often dictates the decisions, and the specific illustration emerges as a total concept. The concept includes what can be communicated with the given technique to physically produce the illustration. The generic view suggested here is of a process of conceptualization, development, and execution, with this process simultaneously measured against the practical considerations of quality, cost, and time. While this process might

seem complex, many decisions in a specific instance become automatic. For instance, cost can determine immediately what method must be used.

Modern technologies allow greater flexibility and freedom than ever before possible. With the current emphasis on offset printing and the use of photographic materials, more can be done and the techniques are less expensive. This should make illustration available to many people who would never have used it under the conditions set by previous systems and techniques. The processes are simpler and less expensive, and with the graphic material available the majority of messages can be illustrated.

The impressive list of categories shown in the chart (1-1) can be expanded with more unique specialties. While it may be convenient to think of illustration in terms of merchandise categories or even in terms of special techniques and points of view—and the system of merchandising illustrations does work in this way—it can also be helpful to realize that a trained artist and illustrator can work in a variety of ways. The illustrator can also deal with a variety of subjects according to knowledge, opportunity, and interest. It is the system of merchandising that determines that an illustrator is known for a particular subject or a particular style.

Because of a sustained market it has been profitable to think in terms of the specialist illustrator. There is the story of the specialist who rendered men's hats and shoes beautifully and who was familiar with all the nuances of changing shape and fashion. He preferred rendering men's hats, however, and he narrowed his specialty because he could get all the work he needed in this area. Eventually this artist could draw only hats, due to prolonged and narrow specialization; and, when fashion changed, with fewer hats worn and the market demand for hat

1-2, 1-3, 1-4, 1-5. Notice the degree of finish of each picture. The category of illustration refers to a specific kind of picture. The pictures become progressively more detailed. Compare the degree of interpretation as well. Contrast the humanization of the woodcarving and the more readable faces in the drawings with the photograph. Illustrations allow greater flexibility of interpretation because the means are less mechanical.

illustration nonexistent, he found himself out of work. The majority of illustrators, happily, are capable of a wider range of work than that of their specialities, the work for which they are known.

The categories are a result of market demand over a period of time, and specialized experience simplifies the work of communication. The experienced illustrator knows the subject and the market involved with the specialty. This enables him to do the work with a minimum of explanation and with a maximum of understanding. A further result of market demand and the mechanical techniques used in a particular market is that certain art techniques come to be preferred. This is because the given technique used can simplify the production process and cut costs.

In the marketplace illustration categories are determined by need, which is the result of the need for communication. The specifics also determine the categories of illustration involved with a particular subject. The needs of the subject and of the reproduction techniques influence the art techniques. For instance, if a sketch is suitable, it is not necessary to go to the time and expense of producing a detailed finished rendering.

Categories of illustration

Each of the specialties listed in the chart (1-1) uses slightly different terminology due to the differences of subject matter. The categories themselves also represent a graphic terminology for the means of verbal communication: one might describe a sketch as being like a fashion sketch, for instance; and it would be distinguished from a sketch by a wildlife artist, in which more exact detail would have to be recorded. Comparisons can be made against a known quantity in an established field of specialized illustration.

A simpler view of the categories of illustration can be obtained by considering them from the standpoint of how much detail is incorporated. This has the advantage of dealing with illustration as an entity and of leaving out the subject matter that it communicates. That these generic categories of art terminology are not precise is understandable. One illustra-

tor's rough sketch may be equivalent to another's finished sketch, for instance. In the practical sense of illustration applied to a particular subject the degree of roughness or finish must be related to the necessary communication, the purpose of the illustration.

To develop this concept in a specific sense, imagine a loose sketch of a garment that overlooks certain stitching details and pockets in favor of emphasizing a fashion silhouette; the sketch would be too loose for advertising purposes, as the public would need to know these details, yet, if done by a designer for a patternmaker, it could be completely adequate with the additional notation "patch pockets here." The usefulness of the sketch would depend upon whom it was for; and, because it depends on whom you are talking to, the degree of finish must be related to the necessary communication and the purpose of the illustration.

When one deals with a specific subject in context, the necessary details are very apparent. Dealing, as we are here, with the generic categories, the illustration can be thought of in relation to how much detail is presented and to the manner in which it is presented. It should be apparent from the preceding example of the fashion designer's sketch for the patternmaker that the patternmaker's drawing also describes the garment but in a different manner.

From the point of view of the manner of the description the garment could be illustrated either by a pattern drawing or by a sketch. The pattern drawing would be more detailed than the sketch. It need hardly be added that only some of us could interpret the garment from pattern drawings. From the point of view of the detail presented we may say that the garment can be roughly illustrated by a sketch, in more detail by a fashion illustration, in still more detail by a rendering, and in even more detail by a photo.

Because we are so accustomed to the use of photos, one might think that one could always use a photo and be done with it. This would be true, except that a great deal of what has to be illustrated and communicated exists only as an idea. If the garment in the example existed, anyone who had to know about it could look at it for themselves, and no picture would be necessary for communication. It can be seen therefore that much communication, and the pictures used for this purpose, deals with ideas or concepts.

The ideas that we have to communicate, whether they concern a garment or a building, are often more conveniently illustrated by drawings, either because the subject is not yet in existence or because it is inconvenient to photograph. A good example of this is the illustration used to prepare a manned landing on the moon. Illustrative renderings were prepared of the vehicles and of the lunar surface—it is interesting to compare the renderings with the actual photos taken later when men were actually on the moon.

There are degrees of variance between the actuality and any illustration. The illustrations of a landing craft on the moon's surface were prepared from available information and required a great deal of technical understanding on the part of the illustrator, as well as artistic ability, in order to visualize the composite of all the information. It appears that the artist's interpretations must always enter into the illustration, which is a graphic representation of the artist's concept. There are subtleties of feeling that emphasize a particular quality and minimize others. These differences of quality usually relate to the subject of the illustration and often require a special vocabulary. Anything that one can invent that communicates the desired quality is an acceptable terminology. It is normally easier to work from an existing picture as a standard and to speak of comparative qualities, such as a looser or tighter drawing, or, in the case of interpretation, perhaps a more somber or a lighter mood. One can think of many descriptive terms, and communication of these qualities to the artist is more exact with a point of comparison to relate them to.

If an illustration must deal with a purely subjective idea, the objects depicted are used symbolically and become a device to convey the information. If mood is the subjective idea to be communicated, illustration can accomplish this with very little delineation of the object and heavy emphasis on the mood. What might be surprising to many is that photography can also be used in this manner, because the photo can be lit, distorted, and manipulated in a variety of ways. The illustration—the photograph—is really an

CATEGORY AREA OF TECHNIQUE

1	APPROACH (Realistic, Stylistic, etc....)
2	MANIPULATION (Loose, Tight, etc....)
3	MATERIALS (Ink, Gouache, etc....)
4	REPRODUCTION (Tape, Film, Print)

1-6. The word "technique" has a number of meanings and is applied to art in a variety of ways. The chart summarizes the text description for easy reference. Each category is a concept.

1-7. With a snap of his fingers this elf can jump out of his shadow. This action makes the point that printing must be done with solid-color ink and that shades of a solid color cannot be printed. If you look at the tonal figure on the right with a magnifying glass, you can see that the tones consist of tiny solid dots, which create the illusion of tone. In comparison the figure on the left is obviously a solid line. Shades of tone made by the tiny dots are produced by the halftone-screen process. The two figures are done in different art techniques and utilize different techniques of print reproduction. If you keep in mind the print techniques of solid line, as in the figure at the left, and of halftone, as in the figure at the right, the art techniques become simple to understand.

object or device separate and apart from the communication that it is intended to represent.

The term "illustration" also specifically denotes a particular kind of picture—that is, an illustration as opposed to a sketch or a rendering. Compare the sketch (1-3), illustration (1-4), and rendering (1-5) shown here; they are arranged in an ascending order of development of detail. A comparison of the sketch, illustration, and rendering with the photo (1-2) also reveals differences of interpretation. If the sketch of the figure were seen by itself without benefit of comparison with the other pictures (cover the others), a girl in a traditional Dutch costume would be communicated. The sketch does not convey any information about surface texture, so we may assume that fabric is indicated. The illustration, taken separately, also conveys the idea of a girl in a Dutch costume. The texture can be interpreted as brushwork, and there is additional information about local color and form: the face is quite completely developed, for instance. The rendering shows all this and also communicates the form and variations of the surface. The garment does not fall exactly like fabric: it looks more like a woodcarving. The photo exhibits the visual texture of wood and shows that this is in fact a carved-wood figure. It does not, however, have the facial niceties and the idealization of the subject.

This example is an indication of differences of subjective interpretation. It shows how pictures are used for communication. The sketch, illustration, and rendering are as much if not more concerned with the subject of the woodcarving, the girl in the Dutch costume, as with the fact that the object is a woodcarving. Lest one think that the photo is automatically accurate, consider that from the photo by itself it would be difficult to say how big the carving is. Photos are not so literal as one might think, because in actuality the carved figure is only about 6 inches tall and is mounted on a doorstop, which is not shown. Because photography is a more mechanical medium, less interpretation is possible.

While these examples help to identify what is meant by a sketch, illustration, rendering, and photo, they do not show the infinite variety of interpretations possible, as one can imagine. They do, however, exhibit the relationships among them,

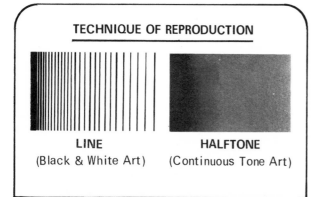

TECHNIQUE OF REPRODUCTION

LINE
(Black & White Art)

HALFTONE
(Continuous Tone Art)

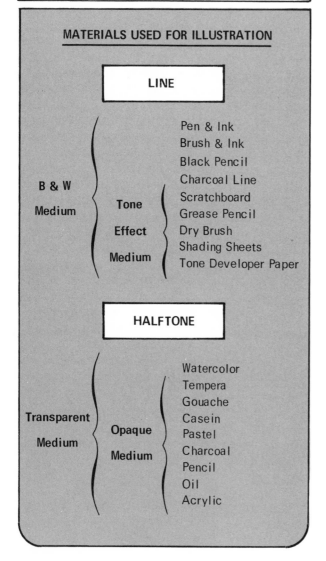

MATERIALS USED FOR ILLUSTRATION

LINE

B & W Medium — Tone Effect Medium:
Pen & Ink
Brush & Ink
Black Pencil
Charcoal Line
Scratchboard
Grease Pencil
Dry Brush
Shading Sheets
Tone Developer Paper

HALFTONE

Transparent Medium — Opaque Medium:
Watercolor
Tempera
Gouache
Casein
Pastel
Charcoal
Pencil
Oil
Acrylic

which can be seen in the amount of detail and in the interpretation. Through the interpretation of the subject one can see the inherent flexibility that allows illustrations to be used to communicate ideas. The limitations are imposed by the mechanics of technique needed to complete the process.

Techniques of illustration

Now more than ever there is an emphasis on uniqueness of technique, which gives rise to great diversity. Illustration techniques are infinitely varied, as much so as is individual thought. The idea of technique is seen in a number of ways, and the word "technique" has different meanings.

To deal with this diversity, it is convenient to invent a conceptual structure to reduce the diversity to a simple pattern. The diagram (1-6) exhibits the pattern. It does not eliminate the variety but is rather a device to supply a useful picture of technique for the purpose of handling illustration. To do this, let us differentiate four meanings of the term "technique."

(1) To view illustration as a device for communication, "technique" is a term applied to the interpretation of the subject; it describes how illustration is approached. An example is to consider a realistic or a stylistic approach, to pick two contrasting approaches to a subject, each of which is a technique.

(2) Moving toward the particular, "technique" is a term applied to what the artist does. It relates to the manipulation of materials or media and to their use in the interpretation of a subject. One may elect the technique (sense 1) of stylization, and this would affect the way in which an artist would use technique (sense 2) to manipulate his or her material. An example of this is the loose or tight drawing already discussed.

1-8. The two blocks at the top indicate a tonal scale, one done in a line-art technique and the other in a halftone-art technique. The materials and methods of manipulation for these two forms are infinitely varied. The chart depicts generic techniques and methods of manipulation.

(3) In regard to the physical use of material the term "technique" includes the different materials or media. Ink drawing and gouache painting are two media. A stylized technique (sense 1), handled in a drawing technique (sense 2) by the artist, and done in pen-and-ink (sense 3) describes a quite specific kind of illustration.

(4) In the application of illustration to a specific use the term "technique" relates to a method of reproduction. The illustration might be used for TV broadcasting, projection viewing, or printing. Each requires a different reproduction technique and entails specific features, such as electronic taping for TV, a transparency for overhead projection, or offset printing. One might specify a stylized (sense 1) drawing (sense 2) done in ink (sense 3) for offset (sense 4)—to continue our example.

Reproduction techniques (sense 4) can be patterned into electronic, photographic, or printed forms. In each form an illustration can be prepared graphically for reproduction. Print is the more demanding because, whereas electronic and photographic reproduction accept variations in tone, printer's ink is but one tone. Printing is essentially a simple on-or-off, print-or-blank process, and black cannot print as gray; the illustration must conform to this requirement, which means that it must be black or white.

If one realizes this fact, there need be no confusion in print reproduction, and it is logical to assume that most of us will be concerned with print illustration, as it comprises by far the largest volume of work. The drawing (1-7) makes the point that, if the art contains tones of gray, these tones must be screened—translated into a series of tiny dots—so that the black printing ink will reproduce the illusion of a tone of gray.

In short, electronic and photographic reproduction can handle line and continuous tone simultaneously, but print must discriminate between the two, because the latter requires the halftone-screen process. Of course, printing is far more complex than a simple on-or-off process, and any type of reproduction more complex than simply aiming a camera. Yet for the user of art it need not be, as a number of specialists handle the specifications of the designer or artist, who need know only the simplest fundamentals in order to avoid unnecessary expense.

The pen-and-ink technique (sense 3), because it is black and white, can be directly reproduced in print. A photograph, because it is continuous tone, must be screened for print reproduction. It is easy to see that art that requires an additional stage in the reproduction process is more expensive to reproduce and that the reproduction technique (sense 4) used affects the art technique (sense 3). Without attempting to be exhaustive the chart (1-8) shows the more popular art materials and their characteristics in the important respect of line and tone.

Because there are many material and media techniques (sense 3), it is useful to consider them in terms of their visual characteristics. The following illustrations show the linear character of black-and-white art (1-9), the textural character of texture tone (1-10), the transparent character of wash tone (1-11), and the solid character of opaque tone (1-12). The characteristics are line, texture, transparency, and opacity, respectively. For print the first two are line art, the second two halftone art.

We know that black-and-white art can be reproduced directly. This also applies to texture tone, because the tiny dots simulate a halftone screen. A litho pencil or, for that matter, any very black pencil used on a textured surface deposits black on the crown of the texture surface, producing a black dot—the bigger the dot, the blacker the tone. The similarity of texture tone to pen-and-ink ceases with any size change, because enlargement or reduction alters the dot structure, making it larger or smaller as well. The size change is therefore limited to the dot size that can be held for reproduction. This is a significant limitation, because most illustration is done larger than the reproduction size. If the dot cannot be held, the art will have to be screened as if it were continuous tone.

The materials used in the four illustrations are handled in the simplest possible technique (sense 2) to show the visual qualities of line, tone, transparency, and opacity. The media techniques (sense 3) used are, respectively, pen-and-ink, litho pencil on textured paper, watercolor, and gouache. In practice materials are often combined to exploit the different effects that each produces.

1-9. This technique is pen-and-ink, perhaps the most basic black-and-white medium. It can give a tonal effect, which shows light and shadow, as well as its native linear effect. The different strokes of pen line produce texture in addition to tone.

1-10. Grease or litho pencil on textured paper is often used for political cartoons in newspapers and in a variety of other ways. It provides a tonal effect yet is a line technique, because the tonal effect is produced by tiny dots on the tine crown of the paper texture. The dots can be photographically reproduced.

Some may feel that transfer and instant-art products represent an entirely new material technique. But these materials must of necessity fit into the categories of visual quality, the categories of line, tone, transparency, and opacity. Transfer materials are cut, burnished, and adhered to the art. It is certainly true that wash tones are achieved without manipulating paint or brush but rather by cutting an adhesive tone sheet to the desired shape. The same can be said of opaque tone paper, transfer images that work as black-and-white line art, and texture sheets that are facsimiles of other art techniques. These illustrations (1-13, 1-14) show the use of shading sheets.

These techniques are gaining wide popularity. They save time and, in the absence of drawing ability, permit better work. They enable an illustration to be constructed with only assemblage skills and a sense of design. In the hands of the artist they can be used for illustrations of all kinds. The work done with these materials, however, must always have a hard edge, since they are manipulated by cutting and tearing. Some photographs and photographic techniques can also be used together with paint. There seem to be endless combinations and possibilities.

The user of illustrations should also realize that the materials techniques (sense 3) can be handled in a great variety of manipulation techniques (sense 2). Each characteristic shown in the previous examples (1-9, 1-10, 1-11, 1-12) can be produced with acrylic paint, which is a very versatile medium. Acrylic gives a linear effect if painted with a fine brush, a wash effect if thinned with water, an opaque effect if used heavily, and a textured effect if used dry on a textured surface. Additional effects of transparency and opacity can be obtained by introducing the medium used in the paint to carry the pigment. Since the acrylic medium for the pigment is a strong, transparent glue, which is waterproof when dry, it allows the incorporation of sand and other unusual materials for textural effects.

Other materials can also be subjected to the same kind of manipulation in order to produce different effects. It is sometimes difficult to tell one from another in the final illustration, and it would take an expert to determine how the effect was accomplished. This is of little importance to the user, because he or she is interested in how the effect "reads"—that is, how the illustration looks.

The repeated design executed in the four techniques (1-9, 1-10, 1-11, 1-12) reveals that not all media lend themselves to manipulation in quite the same way. The reason obviously lies in the way in which the material presents the image as well as the way in which it is handled by the artist. One might compare the clouds in the pen-and-ink version with the clouds in the wash version: it is clear that wash produces the softness of clouds more easily than the hard-edged line of pen-and-ink. The tree trunk is well suited to pen-and-ink and reveals that this technique can be used for both textural and tonal effects, but the shadow area next to the tree is more interesting in the gouache version. The hills in the background of the litho-pencil version have a pleasant texture not seen in the wash version. These comparisons show how media techniques (sense 3) and art techniques (sense 2) lend themselves to some types of subject matter more than to others and that each has a different overall effect.

The great variety of effect is due in large part to the interpretation (sense 1) of the artist, expressed by manipulation of the technique. No two artists even start from the same point of view. To indicate the extent of this difference, it is interesting to observe that it is virtually impossible for one artist to duplicate the work of another, even a simple line drawing done in pen-and-ink. One might think that a line drawing could be traced and that the result would be the same. Try it, however, and you will find that it is next to impossible to start and stop the line at the same points or to maintain the same speed and flow, the same weight of line and pressure. In the final result you can easily register little irregularities and differences, and the drawing and the tracing will look quite unlike. An expert could probably determine which was traced. If one can observe the interpretation (sense 1) in the artist's technique (sense 2) at this simple level, it becomes all the more evident as complexities are added.

The media techniques used (sense 3) also affect the artist's interpretation (sense 1) because of the manner in which the media can be manipulated. It can be seen immediately that the black and white of

1-11. This is a transparent wash done with watercolor. Watercolor is perhaps the most popular tonal medium. Watercolor requires rapid manipulation and thus considerable skill.

1-12. This is a gouache painting. While gouache can be thinned and used transparently to some degree, it is designed as an opaque medium, one that covers the surface so that it does not show through. It is particularly suitable for brushwork and textural effects.

pen-and-ink seems to require more stylization. Opaque seems to lend itself to a more literal and realistic rendition. These differences are relative, however, to the interpretation (sense 1) of the artist and to the use (sense 2) that the artist makes of the media qualities (sense 3). The three areas of art technique interact simultaneously!

To deal with interpretation, broad conceptual structures can be used to relate to the technique (sense 1) in which the subject is approached. Stylized and realistic illustration have been mentioned, and one should be aware of at least these two contrasting approaches. They can be easily recognized. Remember that, since illustration is a graphic device for communication, even very literal photography must present the illusion of three spatial dimensions on the two-dimensional graphic surface. A sense of reality is obtained by using the rules of perspective and by showing the subject in a normal frame of reference.

Stylization often plays with both perspective and the normal frame of reference. If a realistic picture would present too much distracting and nonessential information, it is sometimes far better to use a stylistic illustration that goes directly to the subject and leaves out the distracting information. Styling can be anything that it needs to be. If realism is distracting, the stylizing can often be decorative. A chart, for instance, can be enhanced with a decorative picture of the subject, the simplicity of which would be in keeping with the chart. A realistic approach in this instance might overpower the chart.

If one is familiar with the characteristic features of schools of art such as impressionism or art nouveau, they can be used as conceptual structures to approach the interpretation of illustrative concepts. One

can see illustrations whose visual language belongs to one or another school of fine art. The transfer materials mentioned earlier use a method of application that makes them immediately similar to collage and to the school of art known as dada. Because many sales messages today must deal with intangibles, surrealism is growing in popularity as a technique to deal with the subjective interpretation and the subjective nature of the message.

Whatever the idea to be communicated with illustration, a picture allows greater symbolic freedom compared to the written word. Even if the picture is not used directly to present the idea, it does convey an atmosphere or background that enhances the presentation of the idea. One of the earliest uses made of illustration was to decorate the written message.

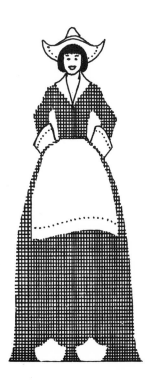

1-13, 1-14. Shading sheets are line art. Each area of the figure at the left, a typical use of shading sheets, is surrounded by a solid line. The figure at the right is a freer rendition of the same idea, using the texture to hold the shape. Shading sheets use shape to define the art; though many textures are available, they do not vary within the shape, as they do in rendered art.

Realism

Art Nouveau

Pop Art

Op Art

Expressionism

Surrealism

EXPRESSIVE

SYMBOLIC

22

2. DECORATION

The art of using pictures to communicate can be viewed even more simply than the many categories of the marketplace. This is how many of us see it, and, while it is obvious, it can be helpful to point out the obvious; the simpler view, perhaps the simplest approach to using pictures, is that of decoration. If one thinks about the function of pictures as a decorative amplification of the idea to be communicated, pictures can be merely embellishment or ornament.

Pictures in this sense are merely added onto the written word. This is a useful view if illustration is limited to decoration. For the moment this is an alternative to the point of view that is commonly held. The use of pictures for communication purposes is not changed—we are merely changing our point of view, our way of seeing. In considering pictures in terms of decoration it is convenient to use the interpretations offered by various schools of art.

2-1. A wheel of distinctive and contrasting schools of art used in commercial illustration should offer a decoration style for every taste. The problem is that such a simple specification does not include all views: use your own interpretation. The point is to work with a wheel of decorative forms.

Everyone sees things differently, and one's way of seeing is a way of understanding. It is a point of view. If a point of view is collectivized around a common characteristic, it is a school of art. The characteristic is a manner, a manner of seeing. This is academic and perfectly obvious, except that we all interpret the manner slightly differently so that, accepting the fact that we do and should have our own opinions about what constitutes a school of art, one may use a characteristic manner of seeing as a way of describing and dealing with illustration.

One can see that characteristic decoration has followed art movements. The movement is a way of seeing, and the ornament exemplifies it. We are considering the characteristic only in terms of decoration for the moment. To illustrate this, we can compare different types of floral decoration. Floral motifs persist throughout art movements: from the acanthus leaves used by the Greeks to adorn the capitol of a column to the daisy that appears in pop art, all make use of floral decoration. The concept of form and the way in which it is used as decoration change with each art movement. Each has a characteristic style in terms of which its decoration can be seen, compared, and used. The decoration changes with the different viewpoints and requirements of different schools of art.

The most important aspect of decorative illustration for commercial use is probably that it appear up to date. One of the requirements for business use is an impression of "now," quite possibly fostered by the intensive emphasis on technology and product obsolescence. If one observes the art forms currently in use, the most outstanding quality in terms of decoration appears to be diversity. It is chic to look different, and it may also be practical, given the volume of material available. The fact that up-to-dateness and diversity may be contradictory makes no difference if one is concerned with fashion.

Art-nouveau motifs are most often used, probably because they are the most easily available and because they are often in line art, which is the simplest art to reproduce. Other popular schools of art are expressionism, op art, realism, and surrealism. These forms are often mixed together for illustration. Is this a new eclecticism, or is it collectively a new art mannerism?

One of the best ways to start an argument is to try to specify and to delineate a school of art. This is a complex and involved task. If you want to argue with the selection presented in the graph (2-1), you are invited to insert your own—if you want to include impressionism, it might be inserted just above expressionism. Whatever your preference, it does not interfere with the point of the illustration, which is to offer a selection of different and contradistinctive schools of art that collectively make up a spectrum of viewpoints.

In the rush to be different many schools of art are represented in illustration. Whichever is selected, it must be among the most popular. At the risk of oversimplification some are loosely defined here to aid in dealing with decorative illustration.

(1) Art nouveau utilizes rules and border treatments to frame and to separate elements of a design in a symmetrical and formal manner. It is often characterized by stark and stylized effects.

(2) Expressionism exaggerates elements in order to facilitate the presentation of an idea or concept. It is often dramatic, sometimes colorful, usually but not always distorted.

(3) Op art involves the use of pattern to produce the image of something else. It is often bold; it plays with the dimensions of space, causing the eye to see depth, then surface.

(4) Pop art uses the commonplace and the obvious but not in commonplace or obvious ways. It is often idealization, sometimes nostalgia; the subject is common but not the viewpoint.

(5) Realism is photographically pictorial, as one might assume. It is often deceptive, because what appears real may be an idealized image of how it ought to be.

(6) Surrealism combines elements in a new juxtaposition in which all the elements can be interpreted symbolically. It often deals with a subjective and dreamlike state that mirrors mental images, sometimes recollections.

Decoration, embellishment, or ornament assumes that the subject matter is primarily communicated verbally. When pictures are used to decorate the written or verbal message, the words convey the specific message, which is filled out—shaded, as it were—by the decoration. The function of decorative pictures is to provide a context, to illuminate the broader meaning or frame of reference. Nonspecific or stylized pictures are added to enhance the message, to increase readability and ease of assimilation. Schools of art, while they apply to a larger area, are a useful device to view nonspecific decoration.

Getting seen and read

In business it is customary to typewrite messages in order to facilitate readability and comprehension. The usual approach is to select a typewriter face that looks efficient and easy to read and, since most are efficient and easy to read, expresses the action, quality, and nature of the business. It is understood that the type should be appealing and attention-grabbing.

At the very outset attention is given to the picture that will be created in the mind of the recipient by the appearance of the message. Typefaces are a sensitive indicator of graphic fashion. Different designs of type can be used to give a distinctive look to the message, and they should be combined tastefully. The drawing (2-2) illustrates the decorative quality of typefaces.

2-2. Type can be used as a decorative as well as a descriptive element. Alphabet symbols can be designed in many styles, forms, and sizes. It is appropriate to consider type as a design element due to its contribution to the overall content of the message. Tasteful use of typography makes a graphically pictorial contribution to the content of the message.

It would be unusual for a concern not to use stationery. There may be no pictures, but the type design and the arrangement of the letterhead contribute to the overall effect. The nature of graphic communication is that it requires an image: the image relates to what is being said by how it is said. In this fashion decoration also communicates.

Decoration becomes more than merely ornament: it becomes a way to enhance and illuminate the literal or actual message with the desired qualities. A letterhead is more than ornament: it shows the firm name and address along with the character and nature of the business activity. Viewed in this way, decoration need not be merely ornament but can also be used as a device to add to the communication. When it is used in this way, it adds dimension to the communication; it makes it more appealing. Making the message appealing is a good way of getting seen and read.

A pleasing arrangement of the message on the page adds to the appeal. Type has a dual role: it conveys the message and also serves as a decoration. The arrangement of the message is used for the sake of clarity, but clarity is appealing: there are many ways to space it on the page. Headings can be used; subheadings can subdivide a message that is more lengthy. The chart (2-3) shows different forms of display. Margins can be changed to set off a particular point. Repeated striking of an individual key, such as the asterisk, can produce a border or frame a heading. Arranging the message involves type in the picture-making process, and the words and letters are used as ornamentation. The illustration (2-4) shows how the typewriter can be used for decorative display.

D I S P L A Y   H E A D I N G S

DISPLAY HEADINGS

```
********************************
*                              *
*      BETTER   DISPLAY        *
*                              *
*       FOR   HEADINGS         *
*                              *
********************************
```

2-3. The pictorial appearance of the message should be consistent with its content, the communication. Headings, which provide display and typographic ornament, enhance the communication. The border on the bottom heading is a decorative typographic ornament, from which there is a great variety to select.

The purpose of type arrangement is to get the recipient to read the message, to prevent the reader from having to wade through a single mass of reading material. Imagine a newspaper without headings—one continuous flow of reading material with no breaks. How many people would read it, regardless of how fast they read? Experts in business-letter writing emphasize the importance of brevity. Advertisers have found that, the shorter the message, the better the chance that it will be read. The use of different levels of headings assists the reader in assimilating the message. Each bit of information is smaller. The headings make the material more palatable and assist the reader in jumping from section to section. If one feels that the reader will miss the message by skipping from heading to heading, one will admit that at least the headings will be seen and read.

It is possible to add to the scope of typewriter headings by using the more decorative forms and larger sizes of transfer type. The illustration (2-5) shows some of the many transfer-type catalogs available. Transfer borders and decorations can embellish and break up a lengthy message. The style of lettering and ornament chosen can also contribute to the message and allow a more individualistic appearance. None of these methods requires any drawing, but they do require planning and a sense of design that simplifies and unifies the message. The use of one or two elements is usually sufficient for decoration. This alone changes the appearance of a piece from that of just another mass of typewritten material. Suffice it to say that the tides and fashions of usage run more and more to individual expression.

By far the majority of decorations and ornaments offered on transfer type are art nouveau in style. This is due to the decorative nature of art nouveau and to the copyright-free availability of some of the designs. Pop art is represented, and some small drawings designed for architectural and engineering use are representative of realism or simplifications of a realistic point of view. Op art, expressionism, and surrealism can come out of the designs.

Making the decoration pull its weight by contributing to the meaning, clarity, brevity, and individuality of the message aids its appeal but is not a panacea. The best and only guarantee of being seen and read is undoubtedly a receptive audience. This requires that the message be viewed from the point of view of the recipient: one must consider the needs of the recipient. This applies as much to the content of the message as to its appearance.

Considering the needs of your reader leads to the realization that your material must be of value to him. If it is of value and if the initial display makes this point, you have a receptive audience—the problems of being seen and read are removed, and that is a panacea. You must now consider the various ways of handling the information in terms of what is appropriate to the needs and motives of the recipient. The content and the presentation become unified from this point of view, and there is the possibility of a more direct approach. Can a series of steps be put into a word diagram? Can a lengthy description of events be tabulated? Can the content be distilled into one image? The diagram (2-6) indicates this process. Simplifying the presentation not only makes the message easier to grasp but easier to remember as well.

The phrase "seen and read" was used for research in advertising readership. An advertisement in a magazine was tested for reader response. The reader, after looking at the magazine, was shown the ad and asked whether it was noted, seen and read some, or seen and read most. A score of 50% "noted" was very good; "seen and read most" was a fraction of this amount. People with a special interest, however, seek out information that pertains to that interest.

It is the synthesis of an idea, the single image, that attracts, and it does not do so unless it has value for the recipient. The additional facts must bear out the initial impression; the message must be consistent. Abstracting the idea from word to image, distilling it into a single image, and presenting an appealing display are the elements of the clearest, briefest, most individual communication. This is the ideal.

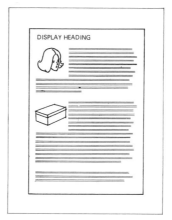

2-4. The pictorial appearance of the message also relates to the physical structure of its display in terms of the sequence of the idea, the emphasis given to paragraphs and subheadings. Pictures can be included to decorate and enhance the message. With management of the pictorial appearance of the communication, the picture symbol easily integrates with the alphabet symbol used for written communication.

Add interest

Decoration adds to the interest of the communication; it helps the reader to perceive what is being said; it makes clear to the recipient that it is in his interest. Managing the material—that is, arranging it, subdividing it, and displaying it with suitable decoration—is essential to communication. As the symbols used for communication are managed, the black-and-white dividing line between written and illustrated communication becomes grayer. Each increase in the management of the symbols contributes to the direct graphic rather than to the indirect symbolic communication and lessens the dependence on the intermediary role of symbol. The advantage of pictures over language lies in its directness and simplicity. A picture is a symbol that communicates spontaneously; language symbols must be translated into images for communication.

2-5. These are a few of the manufacturer's catalogs available from transfer-type manufacturers. They show one-line specimens, or alphabets, and some reductions of complete sheets.

2-6. This word diagram shows the process of expressing your idea graphically. The term "symbol" refers generically to any graphic symbol, so the diagram can apply equally to words or to pictures.

A picture that accurately communicates the intended idea is more interesting because it is more direct than a paragraph of abstract words. The axiom is: if the substance of the words forms a picture, use the picture. One of the easiest ways to do this is to use a diagram. Diagrams can certainly exercise the ingenuity of the originator. The previous diagram (2-6) borrows its symbols from a cartoon strip to make an example. Most people who deal with graphic communication are accustomed to reading a simple chart. In a chart the relationships between concepts can be shown graphically, and it is clearly established that a chart is the simplest and best way to present a relationship between two concepts.

Charts have well-defined forms, and most of us are accustomed to seeing them. Some of the better known are the organization chart, the flow chart, the production chart, and the PERT (program-evaluation-review technique) chart. These charts are used to visualize and to present complex systems. Simpler charts are the line chart, the bar chart, the pie chart, and the pictorial chart, which are used to show the relationships between concepts, as shown in the diagram (2-7).

It is interesting and useful to note that one leg of the chart is often the time frame. This observation can be helpful in preparing a chart. Since charts can be very simply drawn and since many of us have experience in doing so, a chart is a good device to use for communication. Interest is added to the written material by making the idea more graphic, more pictorial. As does tabulating events, it condenses the information, but it improves on tabulation by providing a single image that relates the essential data to the recipient.

It is true that some ideas are more easily handled in words, and, if this is so, words are best. But if the idea should be charted, why is this not done more often? Not because of any difficulty in drawing the chart. One simple way of making a line chart to accompany typewritten material is to use the typewriter to make a grid by striking the period for the desired number of points in a line—12, for example, one for each month—and making the necessary number of lines for the quantity (2-8). The titles and words can be typed in, and, when the paper is removed from the typewriter, the line is plotted and drawn in with a pen (2-9).

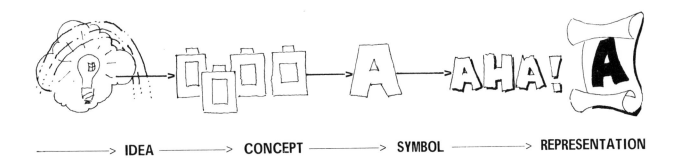

IDEA   CONCEPT   SYMBOL   REPRESENTATION

LINE CHART TITLE

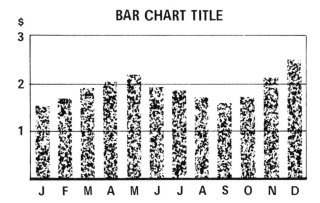

Amount

Curve Label

5
4
3
2
1

Time   J F M A M J J A S O N D

BAR CHART TITLE

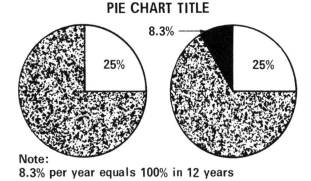

$

3

2

1

J F M A M J J A S O N D

PIE CHART TITLE

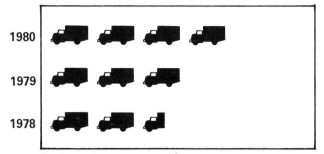

8.3%

25%   25%

Note:
8.3% per year equals 100% in 12 years

PICTORIAL CHART TITLE

1980

1979

1978

Each truck represents 10

The simple charts shown here add interest and have a variety of uses. The line chart shows the relationship between two concepts, often amounts in a time frame. The bar chart is used to show simple fixed values within a time period. The line chart and the bar chart can be combined. The pie chart is very popular for its visualization of quantity and is considered to be the simplest visualization for those who are not used to reading charts. The pictorial chart is similar to the bar chart, except that the bars are placed horizontally and composed of pictorial symbols.

The purpose of communication is usually best served by simplicity. Simpler charts are more easily and quickly understood. Unless the information is designed for experts trained to read a complex chart, it is best to keep charts used to add interest simple. Charts can be made with pictures, such as a map, but with increasing complexity producing the chart becomes work for the artist. A chart specialist is called a chartist.

It is difficult to drawn a hard-and-fast line between graphic display that anyone can do and work that requires a trained professional. The simple charts described earlier can be done by anyone. A choice between a simple and a professional presentation depends on whom the material is for and how it is to be used. Prepared chart material is offered by a number of transfer-product companies. Some of these sheets are shown in the photo (2-10). The prepared material will look the same whether an amateur or a professional puts it down. The difference will appear only in the spacing and in the subtleties of the design. If the design is simple, the amateur can easily achieve a slick, professional appearance. If it takes longer to explain what is needed than to do it yourself, the decision is made

2-7. The four charts here are simple enough for the nonexpert to interpret easily and represent amounts in a time frame. They are made with transfer material, and typing can be substituted for typesetting if necessary. Expressing an idea pictorially offers a number of advantages.

for you. Professionals use the same materials as do amateurs because they save time; by virtue of training and experience they will obviously accomplish the same result in much less time, so for larger projects it is economical to use a professional.

The use of transfer materials yields a new concept of artwork. In the hands of the professional artist they can be used to produce high-quality designs, while in simpler fashion the novice can use them to good effect and produce artwork that once would have required a professional artist. The transfer materials are the alphabets and symbols already mentioned. There are also tapes in different widths, patterns, and colors for making chart lines and bars. Shading and tone sheets can be cut to fill areas, and there is a large variety of arrows, circles, boxes, borders, and ornaments. Manufacturers' catalogs show in detail how the materials can be used, with step-by-step pictures and examples of finished work. One manufacturer, Letraset, offers a workbook that explains techniques (2-11) and a brochure on making simple charts (2-12).

Some people have a seemingly natural dexterity and are remarkably adept at using these materials, which have gained wide acceptance. Business has many uses for graphics, and manufacturing, sales, and accounting make particular use of graphics to transfer and to record information.

The movement of information for business use gives us an entirely new specialty, reprographics. Reprographics may have started with the typewriter but it hasn't ended with the copier, which is just the beginning of a range of machines and materials developed for duplicating and handling information graphics. Communication is the why of it: it is necessary to communicate graphically. It is also necessary to help the recipient assimilate the information overload. More than mere ornament, decoration can be used in this field as a constructive device to be seen and read, to add interest and communication power.

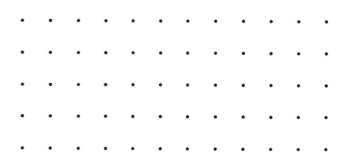

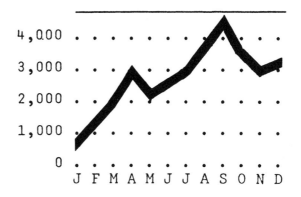

2-8, 2-9. The grid at the top of the chart can be made with the typewriter underscore line. With the heading, quantities, and time frame typed in, the chart line can be added with a pen and ruler or with transfer tape, as was done here. Some dexterity but no special skills are needed for this process.

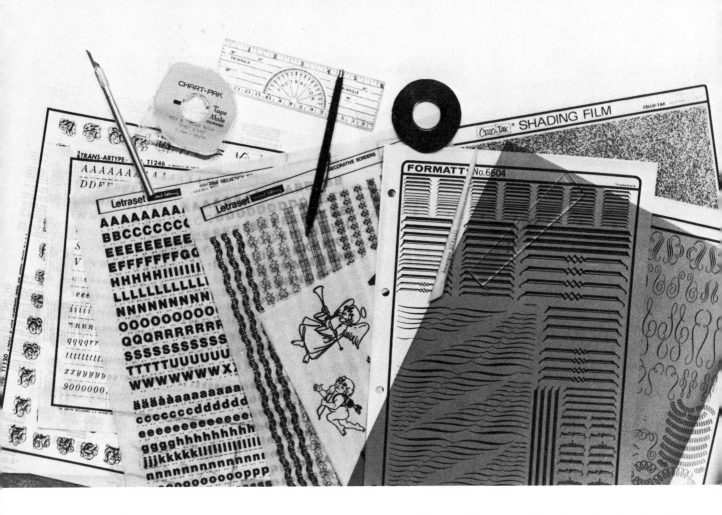

2-10. These transfer-art materials can be used to decorate and to enhance the communication. The novice can use them simply but to good effect.

2-11, 2-12. Letraset offers a workbook (below) that demonstrates how to use its products and offers helpful advice on how to obtain the best results. Most manufacturers offer comprehensive instructions for the use of their products. Letraset also offers step-by-step instructions in the booklet shown at the bottom for basic chartmaking.

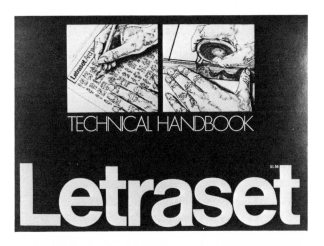

3. GETTING ATTENTION

Pictures can be used as a means to attract attention to a graphic message. Newspaper advertising seems to show that, as the proximity and number of neighboring advertisers grow, so does the graphic size of the heading: it becomes necessary to shout above the competition. The need to have reader attention in order to communicate is clear. It seems natural to think in terms of shouts. Some advertising graphics in newspapers reflect the same idea: there are big, bold, black shouts of typography that make the normal editorial material seem like a whisper.

A picture, such as the drawing (3-1), expresses the same idea, and, since it can be bigger and bolder than type, it shouts even louder. Much newspaper advertising appears to follow the traditional pattern of the marketplace. The dignified broker behaves in another manner in the marketplace—SALE, SALE! SAVE, SAVE! The drawing (3-1) is designed to imply this kind of excitement.

3-1. This sketchy pencil rendering is too big for the page, but there is a reason. It is designed to get emphasis, to shout louder than the competition, to attract attention.

In another environment such as direct mail, in which the message is considered by itself, the requirements are quite different. This drawing (3-2) can afford a lighter touch and can speak in a whisper, because it is viewed singly. The illustration of the rundown apartment building attracts attention by playing against the usual idealistic view for the purpose of encouraging clients to make real-estate listings. HEY, YOU! might get attention but not the right kind.

Once one realizes that attention should be of the right kind in order to communicate, one can think beyond shouting louder. A message can be heard in a whisper if that whisper is attuned to the right ear. Graphics traditionally uses a headline to indicate the contents of the message; the picture illustrates the headline. Both should work together to speak to the interest of the audience. They should be interesting, appealing, and informative, because an audience that is interested is receptive and will focus on the point presented. The point must be true. The benefits must be apparent and believable.

An advertisement that gains attention for its message stands out by its dissimilarity to its neighbors. The art technique contributes to this effect. It is at its

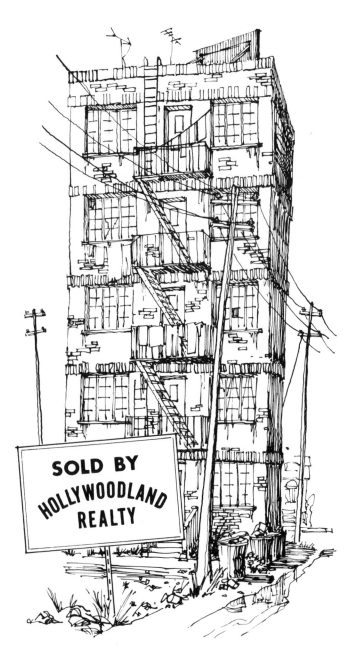

3-2. Shouting louder isn't the only way to get attention. This pen-and-ink drawing departs from the norm and in so doing gets attention. Shouting louder is but one of many ways to gain contrast for the sake of communication.

best when the character of the message is expressed by the character of the graphics: the character of the message *is* the message.

As sound is contrasted to silence, the graphic image is contrasted to the blank paper. The outline of shape and the plane of form are presented by contrast. Contrast is a means of gaining attention. Size, form, color, rhythm, and texture are sounds in the graphic language. The diagram (3-3) shows the principle of graphic contrast abstractly in terms of symbols. It shows that contrast can be exhibited only with a point of comparison. The intent of shouting louder is to stand out from one's environment: the graphic language works in the same way.

In its graphic environment the lead illustration in this chapter (3-1) gains a sense of largeness by contrast with the size of a normal illustration that fits the page. It speaks the language of size in relation to environment. The realty ad (3-2) makes its contrast by presenting the unexpected. Its language is the texture of a line that indicates age.

The choice of the means with which to make contrast can be the technique used to lend character to the art. The art can have a bold character, as in the lead illustration (3-1), or it can have a lighter character, as in the realty ad (3-2); it can have tonal texture or linear texture. A variety of character types is possible. The illustration of the woman shouts; the illustration of the old apartment whispers. Each technique provides an art quality that fits the character of the illustration and of the message. This helps to speed the communication of the message.

With the great quantity of information offered to the viewer the individual gives scant attention to any one advertisement or even editorial message. Selection is a necessity, and audiences are very sophisticated. Attention is based on interest and on receptivity to an idea. With the fleeting span of attention communication needs to be quick and to the point; being noted is not the same as being seen and read.

A message attracts by the content of the subject: the means of communication for print is the graphics, both words and pictures. The nature of the graphic medium requires the use of symbol: words and pictures are symbolic of the subject, not the subject itself. Symbols that represent the subject most accurately interfere least with the idea. Careful use of symbols gains attention and makes the symbols contribute to the message in terms of character as well as of content, and the right appeal to interest transforms the message into communication.

Because of the short span of attention the point of the message not only should be made quickly but, to be seen and read, should make only one point. Some detail may be necessary to the message, but it should concern the same point. There should be sufficient information to complete the point. To do this, the originator of the message may put in a great deal of thoughtful effort. It is surprisingly difficult to say succinctly precisely what is meant. The visual symbols for communication require still more thought in order to attract the viewer's attention.

Graphics for editorial use differ only slightly. The point of the message is different, and more space is usually available. Editorial material is viewed singly. If one thinks of the cover of a publication, however, it is clear that the function of editorial graphics is very similar to advertising graphics because the cover has to get the viewer's attention.

Pictures are useful because they perform the dual function of gaining attention and communicating. They are flexible. They can color the message and present its character speedily. The language of the picture, while symbolic, corresponds to our basic visual experience. This can be used to make the picture an integral part of the message so that it becomes a nearly instantaneous device to make a point.

Through management of the information—composing of the illustration—detail can be focused on the desired point. Whether composition is considered in terms of its content or of the character of its graphic symbols, its purpose is the same—graphics present the idea.

Select the audience

Of all uses of pictures it is a good assumption that the most common is that of an illustration of the subject combined with a heading. Retail advertising commonly shows a picture of the merchandise. Newspapers abound with retail advertising, and

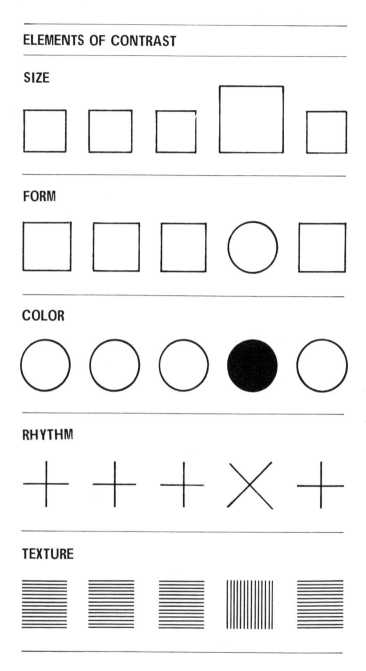

ELEMENTS OF CONTRAST

SIZE

FORM

COLOR

RHYTHM

TEXTURE

3-3. Contrast is a graphic tool that is used in various ways to focus on the subject of the communication. It can be considered in terms of the information within the picture as well as of the relation of the picture to its environment.

CARLOAD SALE

3-4. The heading at left has a number of uses and utilizes both words and pictures to communicate. The gouache painting illustrates and reinforces the words.

there are hundreds of newspapers. Editorial work also illustrates the subject of an article.

The use of a picture in merchandise advertising eliminates the need to explain or describe the subject verbally. The picture acts as an attention-getter and immediately selects the audience that is interested. The heading specifies the service or merchandise offered, and a price is often supplied. There is sometimes a description of details that are not immediately discernible from the illustration, such as quality of material or intricacy of construction.

The illustration tells us the subject of the accompanying copy. It may also tell us, depending on its character, something about the viewpoint from which the subject is handled. For instance, a satirical caricature of a public figure can suggest a critical commentary. The illustration selects the audience that is interested in the subject and also perhaps in

the viewpoint.

This ad (3-4) is an example of a picture that illustrates the heading. It is used strictly for the purpose of getting attention. The subject illustrated is the event—CARLOAD SALE—but it does not definitively select the audience, because it does not show the subject of the advertisement. If the subject were furniture, for example, the heading would have to designate the subject and would read FURNITURE CARLOAD SALE.

The abstract nature of language allows the word "furniture" to cover a large class of merchandise. If the sale included different kinds of furniture, it might be impossible to specifically illustrate all of them. The general heading and the picture would be a way to combine word and image to communicate the idea. If the sale primarily featured chairs, for instance, the role of the heading and the illustration

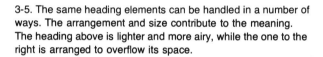

3-5. The same heading elements can be handled in a number of ways. The arrangement and size contribute to the meaning. The heading above is lighter and more airy, while the one to the right is arranged to overflow its space.

could be reversed for better effect. It would be better to show a picture of a chair with the heading CARLOAD SALE. The illustration would select the audience, and the heading would modify the idea.

The word "chair" specifies a general class of furniture, and the audience would have to be told the particular kind—modern or antique, upholstered or wood. The materials should also be described, but they can be shown specifically in a picture. With the subject established by illustration, the heading can play upon the subject, building interest or leading to a focus. Advertising and editorial content both work the same way. No picture detail is necessary for this effect, and a simple illustration works best as an attention-getter. Picture and heading combine to produce an effect, and the application can be used to communicate all sorts of ideas, ideas that go beyond either the picture or the words but are a

result of the relationship between the two. Interesting effects can be achieved by the innovator, and some of the best advertising achieves its effect in just this way. Where words might be cumbersome, the illustration can be specific.

Using a picture of the subject alone allows the elimination of unwanted detail. It permits attention to be focused only upon the subject. This specific focus helps to clarify communication. It can be used to dramatize a point that would be lost if the subject were shown among the distractions of the normal setting. A specific focus gets attention and at the same time establishes the subject, which allows the heading to define it further.

For optimal exploitation of this plan the display medium would also have to be considered. The character and qualities of the subject are best dealt with if the motives of the viewer are taken into ac-

FURNITURE

FURNITURE

Furniture

3-6. The visual display of type also extends content beyond the words, content that helps to communicate the message. The modern, early American, and decorative styles help to indicate which type of FURNITURE the word applies to.

count. We have seen that newspapers have one kind of requirement, direct mail another. Each of the many media is confronted by a different viewer attitude and motive. Is the attitude anticipation or relaxation, one of curiosity or of recreation, a desire for information or for amusement? The communication can be handled better if one considers the frame of mind of the viewer, and the display can be arranged in such a way as to meet his expectation.

That the nature and expectation of the audience affects the reception given to the display implies that the use of illustration should be appropriate. It should be in character with the environment as well as with the subject. If one's own insight can discern what is needed, the traditional view is not necessary, but certain standards have been developed through usage. For instance, heavy, bold designs are characteristically thought to appeal to masculine tastes, while lighter, more airy designs are thought to appeal to femine tastes. While there can be no formulas, a brief look at any medium reveals the conventional standards.

The very conformity of traditional expectations can sometimes be played upon to good effect, as in the realty ad (3-2). It is usually unwise, however, to risk disappointing or offending the viewer. Advertisers have differing opinions and policies in this regard: one famous advertiser claims that public opinion makes no difference to sales as long as the brand is well known; other advertisers feel that the good opinion of the public is important and try to create a favorable image. Whatever your own opinion or advertising need, using a picture to select the audience also lends a personality that is lacking in the cold finality of the printed word. This is the advantage of pictures.

To use illustration to select the audience, then, one considers the character of the subject, the design of the display, and the nature of the audience supplied by the medium's environment. The illustration gets attention and selects the audience, and the combination of heading and illustration in a design communicates. The design provides impact. The display of art and type can either contrast or harmonize. If the display crowds the space, it produces one kind of effect; if it less than fills the space, it creates another kind of effect. The two ads (3-5) show the effects of size. Both designs can have impact, because the impact is considered in terms of how clearly the idea is presented to the intended audience. The design is adapted to the needs of the subject, the display vehicle, and the audience.

The typeface design chosen for the heading contributes to this effect. Each of these three different typefaces (3-6) suggests a different kind of furniture or makes a different kind of appeal. As a rule it is best if the character of the type design reflects or harmonizes with the meaning of the words and with the illustration. The intent is that each symbol used say the same thing, that from all levels the communication is one-directional, and that the effect of the symbols contribute to the same meaning.

There are, of course, exceptions to any rule, and the unexpected can sometimes be used for shock value. It is fun to aim for charming effects, but it is easy to miss. Can you afford to gamble and miss? If not, don't try. It is true that some outstanding advertising does gamble and win, but for big advertisers the gamble is hedged with market research before any big investments are made. The gamble isn't nearly the gamble that it seems to be when you realize that the advertising has been tested in sample markets so that the effects on communication are already known.

Editorial work offers more latitude for the unusual effect. Curiosity is a more important factor, and the impact of the illustration can be backed with factual support if the viewer's interest is arroused sufficiently to read on. In all cases, both for advertising and for editorial work, it would be a mistake to mislead or not to support the illustration immediately with the necessary who, what, when, where, how, or why. And there is also the risk that a normally sophisticated audience would pass by an overly obvious attempt to arouse curiosity if the attractive subject matter were not apparent. Intelligent use of heading with illustration should handle this problem.

As the quality of design and illustration is improved, the opportunity to use art technique for impact increases. The technique of a school of fine art, such as op art, for instance, can be used, and its subtleties can contribute to the communication while specifying the identity of the subject. An effort of this kind involves more design and can be more difficult

3-7. With the heading "CARLOAD SALE" the line drawing of the chair communicates more than the illustration of the truck. Because the drawing of the chair defines the subject, it adds to the content of the message.

to use than straightforward illustration.

Using an illustration of the subject to select the audience implies that illustration specifically represents the subject. Using technique to gain impact also requires an illustration done specifically for the subject, but the carload-sale ad (3-4) shows that the subject can be handled generically. As words specify a generic class, such as the word "furniture," illustrations can also be handled as one example of a class of subject. A picture of a chair cannot be all chairs, but it can be used as an example of a generic class if the heading follows this line of thought. The ad (3-7) indicates this approach. The specific illustration has more impact than the generic, but both are designed to get attention and to select the audience.

Show—don't tell

To describe an event, the axiom for the writer is show, don't tell. The same applies to illustration, although in a somewhat different way, for the function of illustration is to offer a window to communication. For the writer the axiom means to describe and to display the event rather than to interpret it; the picture does just this. The illustration demonstrates the content and ideally lets the viewer interpret for himself. It brings the viewer closer to the reality of the event. The drawing (3-8) shows a subject, the chick, and an event, the chick coming out of the shell—we draw the conclusion that the chick is hatching.

The subject in the context of an event is a complete illustration. The picture tells the story and ideally supplies evidence. Many of us think of photographs as records of events. It is thus natural to present a photo of the subject in the event as evidence. This feeling also contributes to the illusion of reality attributed to a photo. If for practical reasons a photo is impossible, an artist's visualization is substituted. The interpretation is not compared to the reality, but photographers are aware of the difference between experience and a photographic record of the experience.

The picture, whether photo or rendering, turns the subject and the event into graphics, and, though the photo is more mechanically accurate than the rendering, it also interprets. To use symbol requires interpretation. As witnesses give evidence in a courtroom, evidence is given with a point of view. The point of view affects what is seen, even to the extent that there is a possibility of disagreement about the facts.

The point of view affects what is seen; it affects the choice of symbols used to display the subject and the event. As viewers we are inclined to rush past the choice of symbol and to engage ourselves with the relationship that appears to exist between the symbols. As with the relationship between subject and heading, there is also a relationship between the subject and the symbols of the environment shown in a picture.

As we look at a picture, we first seem to want to find the subject—in graphic language the eye goes to the center of interest. This helps us to interpret the meaning. A picture of someone standing in front of a building presents an entirely different meaning than a picture of someone standing beside a building, for example: in the first instance the figure is the center of interest; in the second the building is the center of interest. This is how we would read a picture from the graphic point of view. In comparison, if we were standing next to a building, how might we look at the picture presented in actuality? We might look at either the figure or the building, depending on our subjective focus. If we were to take a picture of what is seen, we would unconsciously select our own point of view as we framed the photograph: we might move to one side or another until we found the record that we wanted in the viewfinder of the camera. The symbols on the film no longer present the full range of possibilities that existed in reality.

We select a viewpoint from which to give evidence. The symbols reflect that viewpoint. The use of symbols in pictures is the same: they must be interpreted. For use in illustration, then, symbols can be selected. In the context of a subject and an event the subject is shown in relation to other symbols. The choice of secondary symbols describes the event. As long as the subject dominates the picture, we see the secondary symbols as relating to the subject.

To recognize the symbolic nature of the graphic image, one can select or reject secondary or associated symbols and in this way compose the picture. One might say that the process is somewhat like framing a picture in a camera except that one moves the symbols rather than the camera. The selection and rejection of symbols in a picture can be compared to writing, to finding the right words to say something. When we feel that the right thing has been said, the composition is complete. A statement has been made, whether literary or graphic.

The picture requires that we show, not tell. Pictures cannot interpret in the way that words can. The elements of a picture, while essentially abstract because of their symbolic nature, are more particular than words. In contrast to an image a word specifically handles abstraction as abstraction: the naming of the abstraction provides the interpretation. If one learns to think of pictures symbolically, one may find little to choose between words and pictures for the expression of a viewpoint; yet, since picture symbols do not interpret the idea to the same degree as do words, it is hard to find a picture symbol for some ideas. Such highly abstract ideas as goodness or pleasure or interest, for example, do not exist as images. We might show relationships that express these abstract ideas: for instance, to show goodness, we might show a little boy savoring an ice-cream cone. The way in which the symbols were handled would convey the idea; but, if the relationship between the same symbols were handled differently, they could also show pleasure or interest. The word names it; the image must show it.

Picture symbols tend to be very specific, but we have seen that they can be made to appear as one of a class, as a generic symbol. The less the detail, the more the generic quality. We have seen that it is necessary to subordinate detail to the focus of the point of view and that this creates impact. There is no formula for managing symbols to get the desired effect, but, if the symbols appear to have the correct emphasis, the composition obviously works. The easiest way to think about this is to imagine that you are a film director and that you have a stage and actors in front of you. Put yourself in their place and empathize: your feelings will help you to identify theirs. Your feelings will also clarify the picture language and contribute to the emotional content. You have the right composition when the stage is set and the players make the right effect.

The usual tendency in illustration is to include too

3-8. More than merely labeling the event, a picture can show it. This pen-and-ink drawing shows a complete event, that of a chick hatching. A heading could slant the communication and focus it on the desired subject.

much. Only the most limited and the fewest symbols are needed to suggest the event. An example might be a basketball player moving the basketball: we can immediately infer that an entire game is going on behind him. The addition of one other hand in the picture would tend to corroborate this assumption. Television, with its closeup shots and rapid movement, has trained us to infer background action from only a few clues.

The benefits of simplification and the recognition of the symbolic nature of the picture have lent greater acceptance to the abstract montage. In this popular kind of illustration symbols are placed around the subject of interest but not necessarily in relationship to the same picture plane nor in any system of unified perspective. Most of us consider illustration as an arrangement of symbols integrated in a system of perspective, such as one sees in a photograph. For a montage additional images are related and composed in a graphically spatial manner in terms of their shapes. In this type of composition, since the relationships among the symbols are abstractly shown, we relate them surrealistically in much the same way as additional facts about the subject supplied with words.

In composing the subject and the event it is best to simplify, because simpler compositions are easier to understand. For this reason simplification enhances the communication. One should, in dealing with visual symbols of the picture, guard against the graphic "split infinitive." One should look for possibilities of interpretation differing from the one intended. This protects against inadvertent misstatement and misunderstanding.

Composition is the arrangement of elements to convey an intended focus and to emphasize one subject. Composition occurs naturally as a result of our viewpoint, as in the example given of framing a photograph. We have a point of view, and we unconsciously try to find a composition that reflects it. We should remember that we can select our viewpoint and should try to find the view that best incorporates the required information. As a rule one should emphasize only one point. This is easily done, for example, by making it the largest.

In the previous examples of furniture one may

remember that it is customary to display furniture in a setting much like a stage set. Showing the furniture in an actual location might show too much accessory detail: for the purpose of illustration the suggestion of a side table and a lamp with a chair or a backdrop of a window and drape supplies enough secondary symbol to give the illusion of the subject in a room. In this context the use of the furniture in the room is the event. The secondary symbols are simply accessories. By making the piece of furniture that is the subject the largest the illustration displays this piece and not the accessories.

Making the subject larger in order to emphasize it is only one way to create a center of interest. The art technique can also accomplish this by making the subject darker or stronger in relation to the rest of the illustration. There are many graphic techniques, all of which show the center of interest in the greatest contrast to its surroundings. Since contrast is the method, the subject can be darker or lighter than its surroundings, larger or smaller, brighter or duller; as the subject exhibits the peak of contrast, the eye naturally goes to it. In the language of metaphor the subject of the picture is the climax of the symbols used to convey the idea.

The composition leads the eye through the picture. We may take in the picture at a glance, but closer observation reveals that the eye actually travels through the picture. The trained artist or designer can to a large degree control this effect and so create a point for the eye to land on. During its travel the eye assimilates information. Though this may last but a fraction of a second, one might compare it to a film sequence. Each subsequent symbol is assimilated and brought to bear on the subject of the illustration.

The figurative language of composition can be exemplified by two tourists: one says to the other, "Stand in front of the building while I take your picture." When the subject takes the position, it is assumed that he or she will be the largest thing in the snapshot and therefore the center of interest. But since there are many ways to make a center of interest, suppose that another figure in the background is coming out of a dark entryway into the sunlight and that the contrast is much greater on this small figure than on the intended subject: the small figure will then become the center of interest. Cropping the picture slightly directs attention even more strongly to the small figure. The ad (3-9) shows this effect.

This ad uses the original (3-1) in a new context. Though it is larger, it directs the eye toward the intended subject, which is the sales event. The heading CARLOAD SALE is the same, but accessories have been added. The ensemble is intended to focus on the event. The activity is the subject, and the woman is symbolic of a participant. A participant of what? The eye travels inward to find out. The answer: CARLOAD SALE.

The picture still illustrates the heading but more strongly. More accessories add to the general feeling and the story. The heading is a label of the event, and the art suggests excitement over bargains. The heading is strong enough for a full page in a newspaper. The words integrate easily with the art because the art is handled as symbol. The art is realistic, but stylized art would have the same effect. To convey the illusion of reality, it is necessary to organize all the symbols according to the rules of perspective. The symbols can also be organized purely in terms of their symbolic effect as a montage.

The heading in the example is a label; the art is generic; no detail is shown that describes particular chairs. The same principles can be applied more specifically if specific content were involved. In a particular situation specific examples of the furniture might be shown; the figure could be a store owner or a salesperson; and the label heading could name the store or a particular day. Again, this would produce a sharper image, and the heading would have more impact.

Editorial illustration can be handled in just the same way: the only differences lie in the content and in the way in which the subject is handled from the point of view of its meaning. Label headings are useful, but a specific image of the subject and the event helps to define a label, and the heading can then amplify the meaning of the label from a particular point of view.

CARLOAD

3-9. These are the same elements used previously but now in the context of chairs. Though nonspecific in terminology, the picture extends the meaning with more detail and with an arrangement designed to lead the eye into it. Specific personalities, time, and place would complete and focus the communication.

R van Uchelen

4. PRESENTING INFORMATION

The most important aspect of illustration is its content, for it is the content that contributes to the communication. As one deals with the presentation of information, one is concerned with communicating the idea. The more important part of the idea is the quality that it presents. Illustration presents both an objective idea, the subject, and a subjective idea, the quality of the subject.

The subject is interpreted from the graphic symbol. Its quality is interpreted from the way in which it is presented. The graphic symbols therefore supply information about the subject in such a way as to lead ultimately to the subjective interpretation. This is a point of view. Since it is unlikely that graphic representation can supply all the information about a given subject, the point of view both selects and edits information.

The point of view helps to present information by selection because it reveals the information. In other words the way in which you look at something determines what you see. The point of view is an attitude. It disposes one to see certain qualities that comprise the information. It directs one to a physical view of the

scene, as in looking through the viewfinder of a camera, in which the desired information is included. The information is expressed in terms of shape and form,

4-1, 4-2. Comparing the picture at left with the one at right shows how the same scene can be viewed as different in content. Each picture presents different information about the same subject.

line and plane, light and dark, and other graphic symbols that communicate facts about the subject. The point of view selects the facts, which in turn reveal the subjective interpretation. As shape and form are different aspects of vision, atmosphere and emotional content are ideas that are revealed in the use of graphics to reflect a focus of vision, a subjective viewpoint. The viewpoint goes beyond the mere recording of data. In the relationship of ideas is seen the art form; in their qualities is seen the art.

Such concepts can be difficult to visualize in abstract language, but an illustration may clarify them. Although in preparing an illustration we move from the viewpoint through the selection process to the particular, in reading an illustration we move from the particular to the general. The lead drawing (4-1) exhibits different textures. We read the textures as shapes, the shapes as trees and their shadows. This is the objective content of the picture, the subject. Through the relationship between overlapping tree and shadow shapes we perceive the feeling of light and shadow. This is the atmosphere or emotional content. One interprets this feeling according to one's own image of the play of light and shadow. The feeling of light playing through the leaves of a tree can be shown in many ways. It is a general idea, but the drawing represents a particular point of view.

One can look at a scene either as a pattern of shapes or as objects in space but not both at the same time, because each exhibits a different dimension, a different viewpoint. Different ways of seeing reveal different information. Seeing pattern reveals shape; seeing space reveals form. Shape shows differences of depth and perspective. Tone and texture relate directly to the two dimensions of graphics; depth and perspective must present a graphic illusion of a third dimension. As far as choosing which viewpoint to use for illustration is concerned, one is no more real or valid than the other. Both express a viewpoint; both are ways of seeing that have graphic counterparts in the symbols used to represent them. Each viewpoint reveals different information. viewpoint reveals different information.

The drawing (4-1) patterns trees in a park. It presents the quiet activity of different textures, one against another. It represents a point of view, a way of looking at the scene in which textures predomi-

nate. The painting (4-2), by comparison, exemplifies a different way of seeing the same scene. Light and shadow form a third dimension, and the same trees seem to be an umbrella of shade from the light and heat of the sun. The dog emphasizes the activity and the depth of the scene. The communication is one of warmth and coolness.

Each individual interprets the principal elements slightly differently, but the two illustrations of the same scene clearly communicate two different ideas as a result of two different points of view, which in turn reveal different information and consequently convey a different atmosphere and feeling.

Atmosphere and feeling are the mysterious elements of illustration that are supposed to baffle the layman. While it is true that the professional can interpret more fully than the novice, anyone can understand the logic of a picture. Indeed, for illustration to work as communication, there has to be understanding. If one understands that the communication is a result of taking a point of view, which works in practical terms as a way of seeing, the logic becomes very apparent. Since illustration can be very simple, as has been shown in the use of the subject alone, great intellectual gymnastics are not involved. A normal, natively intuitive approach perceives the obvious.

The manifold ideas and individualistic, subjective interpretations of atmosphere and feeling are indeed very subtle, but to present information and direct feeling are not complicated. If, for instance, we would disagree about the exact temperature indicated in the painting (4-2), it is of no consequence to the central communication: we can agree that the sun is shining because of the shadow, that it is warm, not cold, because the trees are in foliage, and that we are standing in the shadow as we view the scene, because the shadow is in the foreground. This presents sufficient information for subjective interpretation for most purposes of illustration, and there is no need to psychoanalyze the subjective quality. One's own spontaneous assimilation will be similar to that of others.

To present information, the following elements of the "language" of illustration are used: pattern, space, shape, form, texture, light, line, tone, and color. These visible qualities in turn suggest the at-

4-3, 4-4. Is it a family album? The large head of the woman seems to relate to the other three as we seek to interpret the pictures. The fact that we immediately look for a common theme is the point, and the connecting link between all the pictures becomes the communication.

mospheric qualities that provide emotional content. Information is discerned on each level through illustration. The illustration evidences the idea through presenting the visible qualities, and we interpret the content of the subject from the relationship of idea to environment. The illustration can be light or dark, bright or dull, obvious or mysterious, happy or sad; it can present an entire range of feeling as well as data to support the feeling. The feeling presented by the illustration contributes to the information and is the result of a point of view. Idea, environment, and interpretation are the collective content of the picture.

When one takes a viewpoint in working with pictures, it selects from the myriad possibilities the particular ideas that best express that point of view, and the quality of the ideas suggests which visible qualities to use. The painting (4-3) expresses a viewpoint by taking a high angle of the subject. To present information, one chooses the angle or perspective that best focuses on the information necessary to the story. This unusual angle emphasizes the gesture and contributes to the mood, information that helps us to interpret.

While it is subjectively possible to look at every face as if it were the same and is a viewpoint, it is not possible in reality. This point of view might be shown graphically as a face in shadow, with little definition of detail. But every personality and situation is uniquely particular. Though we use the same word, "face," for every face, each face is particular in graphic terms. Illustration is better suited to show this fact than is language. The particularizing of detail possible, though not unavoidable, with pictures is a way to present information. It is characteristic of graphic picture language. Each of these three faces (4-4) is distinctly different. The graphic language can be generic or specific.

Just as the individual statement in language is a sentence and as we can combine sentences to make a paragraph, so the individual statement in graphic symbols is a picture and we can combine pictures to make a montage. The montage can be thought of as a number of views worked into one composition, as previously explained, but it can also be considered as a collection of separate pictures with a common theme. The four faces (4-3, 4-4), considered as a unit, illustrate a montage of pictures composed on a common theme—in this case faces. By contrast and emphasis the picture group can tell a story greater than the sum of its parts. One sees the pictures in a group context and carries the information conveyed by one into the next so that they relate collectively and present an idea. In the example, for instance, what is the relationship between the dominant woman and the other three people? We know how they are used in our example, but in another context the relationship could be the story.

The comparison made between the two illustrations exemplifies another way of using more than one picture to present information. The comparison between the two pictures makes the idea of viewpoint more apparent than does either alone. The use of more than one picture works in a similar fashion to the use of a single picture in which the subject is placed in an environment. Each additional picture is similar to adding detail to a theme: the difference, of course, is that each detail is a complete picture, while the theme is the subjective idea that connects them.

Reporting

To use pictures for reporting is to use pictures to present information—one wants to know what the picture is saying. The simplest format is an illustration of the subject alone; the next simplest is the subject in an environment. Even the subject alone has content, because we interpret the character of the subject. The environment adds to the scope of the content. In presenting information the picture content is the important part of the illustration. In reporting the picture content can be the subject, because the content can indicate an idea or meaning, which is the story, outside or beyond the picture.

The point of view makes the content, and, in the case of a story beyond the picture, the point of view becomes the content. Consider the photo (4-5), a picture of a manhunt. Beyond the police lines a fugitive is hiding in the shadows. The police are the center of interest within the picture, but the viewpoint leads one beyond the picture boundary to the focus of the police activity, and the fugitive becomes the subject, even though he or she is not seen in the picture. Again, consider the different quality that the picture would present if it were shot from the other

4-5. An event such as this one always draws a crowd—what is happening? The report of the picture draws attention to the subject: it is a manhunt, and the subject, the man being hunted, is beyond the picture frame.

side of the police line: the change in viewpoint, both in the objective view of how we see the police line and in the subjective view of its implications, would drastically change the meaning of the picture.

When one thinks of the subject of a picture, one spontaneously includes the subjective content. When one interprets, the meaning amends the purely graphic focus and directs thought to the subject in terms of meaning. As we view the picture, we combine both the subjective and the objective elements through interpretation. Interpretations are imprecise to a degree, as are the meanings of words. The way in which one uses words provides additional coloration and meaning. With a picture the way in which one uses symbols likewise provides additional coloration and meaning.

Central to meaning is the point of view, and in reporting one is giving evidence in a manner of speaking. The trained observer tries to objectify his point of view and to report without bias the fact that is seen. But since any physical observation point involves a physical point of view and since any subjective interpretation predisposes the observer to select the observation, it helps to know your own point of view. One concludes that, short of omniscience, one will introduce a viewpoint. Trained observers recognize their bias and make efforts to compensate for it. Understanding one's viewpoint helps one to use its perspective as an aid to communication by reversing the polarity and correcting the bias.

It is often convenient to use photography for reporting because of the speed with which a photograph can be made. Accepting the fact that each point of view reveals something different, one searches one's own subjective view for understanding and tries to locate a physical point of view that will reveal the desired information. This helps to explain at least some antics of press photographers. One must always bear in mind what the picture is saying and whether it is true in relation to the facts as the photographer understands them.

The nature of photographic illusions is illustrated by a photographic trick in which someone seems to be holding a figure on his or her hand. The individual who is to do the holding stands close to the camera, extending his hand palm up; the figure to be held stands at a distance in the background; the photographer aligns the palm of the near figure's hand with the feet of the distant figure so that the distant figure seems to be supported by the hand. The illusion is increased if the near figure appears to be making some effort to hold the distant figure but even if corroborating information is added, the graphic image is pure illusion, not fact.

Art can say what photography cannot, because it is a more controllable medium. Capturing an accurate graphic representation can sometimes be very difficult. To photograph an oil spill, as opposed to painting it (4-6), the photographer must look for the characteristic refraction of light on the surface and locate the light at just the right angle to show all the colors. The birds won't pose at all! An oil spill cannot be seen to any great extent at the surface level, unless it were to gush upwards. Deep water prevents this, and the blowout beneath the water has to be viewed from above for the oil to be seen at all. The oil will not be dramatically visible until it reaches the beaches. It is easier to arrange the composition in the painting, because the artist can move the elements around to suit. It is necessary to use them in such a way as to make the content clearly visible.

It may seem curious to consider a pictorial representation of a disaster in terms of composition, yet it is the composition that makes the communication, for it expresses the viewpoint. Whether the subject is beauty or disaster, the same rules of composition apply; considered without the content, even a disaster must compose a graphic display, so there is a conundrum of a beautiful display of the grotesque.

Both photography and art have the capability of reporting, but each presents different problems in providing a picture of the information. In the example of the oil spill it is possibly easier to get the necessary tonal contrast with art. Since the veracity of the painting is corroborated by the oil washed up on the beaches, the believability of a painting is no longer a problem.

The different quality presented by the various techniques should be considered. One sometimes cannot see the forest for the trees, and getting a photograph of a single tree is next to impossible. Again, art would be a solution, but in the case of trees a drawing would present the character of the subject better than would a painting. Compare the effect of the photo with that of the drawing (4-7). The linear quality relates to the content, as does the tonal effect for the painting (4-6).

One should also consider the size at which the art will be displayed. The city photo (4-8) relies on visual texture to present the subject: too small a display destroys the image presented by the texture, and one is left with only the tonal pattern. Imagine that one had seen only the small picture: the impression of the content would be entirely different.

Each of the preceding examples requires a certain amount of detail to make its point. The oil spill needs the tonal variations on the surface, or it would merely be a picture of a drilling platform; the forest needs the linear individuality of the different trees; the cityscape needs the shape of the texture to show the buildings. The subject is also best viewed from one angle, and the composition is designed to bring out the content. The composition includes the manner in which the subject is displayed. The intent of reporting would predetermine the approach to the composition, and the viewpoint would select which details were necessary to the content. The examples relate to the basics of tone, line, and texture and collectively indicate that a particular graphic quality dominates the information to be reported. This is often the case, and the sacrifice of secondary quality strengthens the communi-

4-6. We find the artist's interpretation less believable than the photographers. Art should be used with a view to communication, because its ability to explain is more important than its believability. Taking a photograph that conveys the same information as does this illustration would be quite difficult.

R. van Uchelen

cation of the intended point. Since one cannot say everything, it is better to say one thing clearly.

When the story cannot be said with one picture, one can use several. The difficulty with additional pictures is that they use space and therefore must be smaller in size. The impact of any one picture is diminished. Choosing one picture to be dominant, or to be the lead picture, as it is often called, improves the composition and the communication by emphasizing the one point of view.

The four photos (4-9) collectively tell the visual story of climbing into the mountains. The peak of the mountain is the natural focal point, and this picture is the largest. Whether for a single picture or a group of pictures, one should always choose the extreme point of the action or movement for emphasis or display. The device used to demonstrate the climb

is the timberline: the series starts with small trees at the beginning of the line, goes through the panorama of mountain peaks, displays the highway and its elevation, and reaches the tall, sparse trees at the top, with a vast, distant landscape behind them. The pictures are arranged in reading order: the viewer moves from left to right in two rows. The edges of the shape made by the four pictures is irregular, adding interest with the surrounding white space. They could also be arranged so that they formed a rectangle and no space was left around them. In this case the subject is nonspecific as to locale for the sake of illustrating the use of multiple pictures on a theme, but the introduction of a particular subject, such as a mountain cabin or the name of a road, would immediately particularize the theme.

Grouping of pictures is so common that it does not

4-7. The pen-and-ink technique in the illustration at right can show a scene that cannot be photographed because of the proximity and lighting of the forest, as seen above. The interpretive illustration better explains the view.

4-8. In selecting a technique and an illustrative approach one should realize the effect that the size of the display has on the subject matter. At a reduced size the meaningful texture of the city is lost, and the clouds become the most important feature.

require much explanation. Whether the pictures are placed in one group or extended through several pages depends on the space allowed. It is sometimes more economical, especially with color, to place the pictures on one page: this allows the negatives and the mechanical work with the pictures to be handled as one unit and lowers costs. It is sometimes preferable as well to present information by relating the pictures closely: as a montage the pictures may collectively tell a story that would be lost if they were displayed separately; if the pictures are to be used in a small size, they may have more impact in a montage grouping.

Selling

When using pictures for selling purposes, one attempts to display the product to advantage. Selection of a point of view is carefully considered, perhaps more so for selling than for reporting. In selling the product's qualities and advantages are the story; but, more than merely presenting the story, it is slanted to the market and to the buyer's interest.

Selling is considered here as uncovering and presenting product qualities and then finding and displaying this information to the particular market that needs and wants the product. The selling function is to present the information to the market in terms that the individual buyer will find to his benefit. The product can be tangible or intangible, a manufactured article or a service, each of which requires a different presentation. One can also present a new product to a business—professionals dealing with professionals—or a program to a civic organization—nonprofessionals dealing with nonprofessionals, which also entails different requirements for the use of graphics. Selling from this point of view is something that most of us engage in, and it is considered here in the best sense, as the service of aligning supply with demand.

To present sales information, it is customary to consider the product or service in terms of its ideal and to consider it specifically in terms of those qualities, those parts of the whole, that meet a specific need practically. While we are accustomed to idealized presentations that minimize or even exclude certain objectionable realities, one must ensure that leaving some information out does not misrepresent the product or service. The presentation and the use of pictures for this purpose demand idealization, but this must be done within the standards and norms of usage, and the idealization must be factually supportable. Public presentations that go beyond these standards are subject to prosecution, business-community censure, or both. And the customer who is disappointed by claims that are not supported by fact never returns.

All levels of pictorial quality are usable if the application is suitable, but, in order to acquire an illustration or photograph of the product suitable for sales presentation, it is almost a necessity to use a professional artist or photographer. In comparison with other sources of pictures this may seem expensive; but, to be effective, suitable work is required, and the costs can be defrayed by repeated use of the picture for various graphic displays. In selling a product it is usually necessary to have a picture of the specific product. Selling intangibles presents a different problem, and various illustrations can be used symbolically to express what is wanted pictorially.

In using pictures to sell it is important that the points that the picture emphasizes be well considered in terms of the market to which the picture will be displayed and that these same points work for other intended applications as well. This is the point at which a picture for selling, an advertising illustration, may be better considered than one for editorial presentation, in which the use is not so extended.

A knowledge of markets, sales points, and customer demand is the salesman's expertise; and, though an experienced advertising artist will be familiar with these points of view, he or she should be supplied with specific information on the quality, purpose, and market to which the illustration will be directed. The artist in all probability does not have the depth of understanding and expertise that the sales specialist has about his own products.

It is the nature of the salesman's viewpoint to see his product in terms of its ideal: he is the last to see very slight imperfections, because, having handled so many examples of the same product, he tends to look at the individual product generically as one of a type and this type is the ideal. Products selected for photography should be the very best examples, free of minor flaws that do not represent the ideal. For a rendered illustration the ideal of consumer demand should be described to the artist, without interfering with his own contribution to this view. The products pictured are often not mass-produced but rather handmade, with every element made to the best tolerances, something that might never happen during the production run. This is idealization, but the public is accustomed to this kind of presentation and in fact demands it: it is the norm to present the item in its best possible light, consistent with factual design standards.

It is perhaps this usage that is responsible for the predominance of photography. It is customary for an architectural rendering to show a structure fully landscaped against a cloud-swept sky: nary a cloud shadow is cast on the structure, and there is always glorious weather. Does anyone ever ask how the building looks in the rain or against the snow? Never. It is acceptable for perspective to be dis-

4-9. Synergism—the concept that the total effect is greater than the effect of each separate element—characterizes a photomontage. This series of photos leads us to the top of the mountain.

torted slightly to enhance the design appearance: a new car is shown longer, lower, and wider, and the art is actually longer, lower, and wider than the product—if buyer demand requires it. But photography is more real, more convincing than art, or so it was believed until the public began to realize that models used in automotive ads could not be over 68 inches tall and that the camera lens could distort as easily as could the artist's rule. The fact is that both photography and illustration present a point of view.

The most effective presentation expresses a single point of view. Because of this it is best to select from many possible sales features the single feature that is most important for the market to which it is being presented. A pictorial presentation that incorporates more than one emphasis has no emphasis, and too many sales points can be as difficult to read as are classified ads.

The point of view used in the graphic presentation leads to the story told in the advertising message. Most advertising presentation is designed to interest the buyer in making further inquiry. But some advertising, such as mail-order, must do more than this—it must close the sale. This is more difficult and requires anticipating and answering the buyer's questions. There are also sales proposals that require the presentation of a great deal of information. The more information that can be graphically presented as a picture, the easier it is to assimilate. Once the buyer has assimilated it, he can then compare and make judgments. As buying information and merchandising systems become more complex and provide less human assistance, art and the use of the graphic image become more important.

When presenting an idea with a picture, no matter how much detail is incorporated, every effort should be made to make the main idea stand out clearly. The detail is then subordinate to the main focus of the picture. More ideas need more pictures. With secondary pictures the composition should indicate a single main idea so that the pictures have a theme. The handling is very similar to that of an editorial or a report, except that the purpose is to sell.

Selling intangibles requires that the picture be symbolic of the product. This is not so literal as a pictorial presentation, and it calls for imagination and

4-10. These photos show a series of mental stages in the process of determining a product display. In these stages the product qualities are isolated, and the best way to explain the important points graphically evolved.

evaluation of the secondary effect of the symbols chosen. The literal meanings of the symbols should not interfere with the message or be tangential to the main point. It is often the coincidence of the picture and the heading that conveys the message. Whatever device is invented, it must be primarily clear in its meaning, and the symbolic atmosphere should be harmonious with the message. For illustration it is sometimes best to use a common symbol rather than an original one simply in order to ensure communication: with this the communication can be original. Knowledge and judgment are obviously needed.

To focus on some particular problems of graphic presentation, let us consider the presentation of a widget. Since no one has ever seen a widget, this situation is similar to that of introducing any totally new product. Because it is totally new, it is not necessary to use that most used word—"new"—to differentiate this widget from other widgets that have

been seen before. The problem is one of making the widget understandable in terms of ordinary knowledge, which is more difficult.

Almost anyone, when first seeing the widget, will wonder what it is. To explain this with a picture, we must show its properties, its qualities. Since the reader is not yet aware of these either, this example will make plain what experts can often forget when talking to the layman who has no previous exposure to the subject—to start answering questions at a simple level.

The first photo (4-10a) of the widget, the usual three-quarter view, presents its shape and form. Its appearance is rectangular; it is shaped like a building. Beyond this its texture, substance, and size are difficult to make out. As we look for a better display, it is apparent that a background, an environment, will help us see that the widget is transparent. This improves the presentation (4-10b), but the form is still not clear. A high angle that shows three sides

with a background may help (4-10c): it is better, but the transparency is confusing. A dark background contrasts better if the widget is properly illuminated to appear as a light-reflecting object against the dark. Transparency and light reflection are very difficult to deal with. By changing the angle slightly we can now see the form, the smooth surface texture, the transparency, and what is going on within the widget (4-11a). We know the physical characteristics; we know what the widget looks like as a physical object. We may suspect but do not really know the size of the widget until we have a known quantity to relate to: the hand and the pen (4-11b) give scale, but, because widget. The next step would be to show the widget in use in order to better understand its purpose. The object used for these examples is actually a manifold machined out of solid plastic, which is used to distribute fluid in a machine. When not in the machine, it makes a very interesting paperweight.

The human figure is often used to provide scale

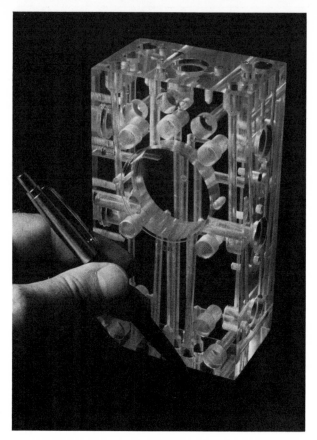

4-11. The photo at left defines the product's qualities in the most desirable way. The hand in the photo at right, while giving scale, detracts from the product.

and situation for objects. As one develops the presentation, one needs more and more expertise for the display of the information. Showing the subject in use in an ideal setting may be best, but it is also most expensive. It requires professionals, models, stage settings, lighting, equipment, and the expertise to coordinate these elements.

The two drawings of the hand truck (4-12) illustrate a simpler presentation and the use of multiple pictures. The line drawing of the hand truck might be difficult to understand alone, but, shown in use, the design for going up steps with a heavy object is clearer. If a simple drawing of the hand truck in use were shown alone, however, one would not know whether the object of importance were the man, the barrel, or the hand truck. Both pictures together make the desired emphasis.

Simple symbolic art, such as the plane and truck shown as a black silhouette (4-13), can be used to present an idea. Because the plane and the truck resemble nothing specific yet present the quality of a plane and truck, we can read them generically as symbols. They have a transportation theme in common; they illustrate something dealing with transportation. Transportation is a generic idea, an intangible.

The use of pictures to present information is really limited only by the imagination. All kinds of presentations are possible to the imaginative user. Professional help is a telephone call away. Costs and budgets determine the scale of presentation that can be entertained, but pictures convey the message easily and are readily available, perhaps more so than is imagined.

4-12. Two pictures, line drawings, explain the product. Either drawing by itself would not provide sufficient information.

4-13. Abstract symbols convey the idea of a service. The plane and truck are not particular, and the triangular shapes in the center suggest an hourglass. The element of time in connection with the plane and truck might suggest speedy delivery.

4-14.

This view of the ocean, although realistic, can be used symbolically. It is used here as a symbol for the word "source."

SECTION II:

SOURCE OF ILLUSTRATION

5. DESIGN CONCEPT

The metaphor of the ocean stands for the vastness of thought. The source of thought and the source of idea are what we reach out to when we need a concept for a picture. Behind the concept is an idea, but the concept of the idea is the form that we work with. Each individual has his or her own ideas: if you can write about the subject, then you have your own ideas about it, and ideas are very individual. Concepts, on the other hand, can be used to display the idea. They can be the framework for communicating.

The design is the mental image of an action or thing and is distinguished here from the essential individual idea. The design concept is a device to represent the idea. Because of the individuality of ideas one's own way of communicating is also highly individual, though the concepts used might be the same as those used by another. We may say that a principle is universal and that therefore anything derived from it is the same, but each application is unique, and the idea is individual. It follows that the concept expressing the idea is always handled differently. An example of this is the same assignment given to ten different artists: each artist will present an entirely different picture of the same subject.

As an individual in search of a concept it is useful to think on paper. Some people find blank paper a screen on which to visualize images, and they just sit and look at the blank paper, rearranging images mentally until they find the one that they want—then they draw it. It is necessary to make this observation because mental activity and physical immobility can be disconcerting to someone who expects something to happen yet sees no physical activity. The kind of individual who is intimidated by blank paper may be more adapted to our society, because he or she must be more active physically. This can be construed as the equivalent in art of wearing hard-heeled shoes and moving around smartly. If blank paper scares you, draw doodles: just about anything will do. The scribble (5-1) is an example made by starting with a certain kind of line: as the lines multiply, images start appearing. It is something like reading inkblots. In whatever manner you work both methods accomplish the same thing: they put the individual in touch with his own imagery. The individual who uses blank paper is merely more consciously in touch with this capacity.

5-1, 5-2. The scribbles in the background are a device for getting the creative flow started. They take one's mind off themselves and engage it in the task of finding images. The chart describes the steps leading from idea to communication.

Design can't be categorized, yet with this categorical statement we can examine the flow that produces a design, realizing all the time that the experience is different from the observation. The word diagram placed on top of the doodle sheet (5-2) shows the flow of thought: it can be read from top to bottom in the mainstream but also across and crisscross. The diagram assumes that you have your own ideas and that you know what you want to communicate, to advertise, or to report. Starting at this point, the design-concept-development process flows through to the conclusion: it starts with the subject, its association or inference, and ends with the communication, which is the object or purpose.

Depending on how one thinks, associated ideas are a useful beginning. This is similar to free association in psychology, in which, if someone says "blue," the associated response might be "sky." Such association is a discovery process that is sometimes surprising in its results. The more analytically minded can successfully pursue logical methods of inference to discovery. These methods yield an image that can be indirectly metaphorical or directly symbolic. Through association or inference this image is seen in character with the subject. With the connection of the image to the subject apparent to you, you must now connect it with copy or accessory for the viewer. The tableau is then arranged to provide the proportionate emphasis or focus. It is at this point that visualizing on paper is essential, because most of us are not able to sustain mentally all the detail of the image that we wish to present, let alone arrange it. Even the most experienced designers need at least a symbolic device to manipulate the elements of their design.

Because every artist works differently, one should try different combinations according to one's own preferences in following this diagram. In this fashion one can find the flow of one's own thought. One must remember that each situation also has inherently different demands. By confronting a practical problem with which one is familiar the steps to a design conception fall into place. The practical requirements and one's own knowledge of them turn one's attention to the objective, and the steps generalized here fall into a useful pattern.

The conceptual framework of schools of art may seem useful; but, though they are ways of seeing, they do not automatically produce images. They are not sufficiently particular to do this, but they can be used as a starting point from which to approach the subject. One can infer images by imagining how the subject would appear in the viewpoint of a school of art. From this point the design process would be the same as before.

Layout

It is possible to think in the most creative terms in picturing the idea to be communicated. This is always a good way to approach the subject, in spite of considerable limitations that must be taken into account later. The reason is that it is easier to cut down the scope of the concept than it is to expand it. Yet the practical limitations must also be dealt with—the budget, the resources for picture making, the needs of communication. What must be presented has to take priority over the luxury of attractive detail.

For thinking and planning it is very convenient if you draw your ideas. One can think on paper, exploring the idea graphically and in images. This helps you to find the desirable image. It may only be in concept form, but for layout purposes an image is easier to deal with than an abstraction. This thinking process is the preliminary stage of concept development and is necessary before a layout can be made.

The layout is the blueprint of what is to be built. It suggests the image and shows the relationships among all the parts. If a layout is not actually drawn because it is felt that the design is so simple and conventional as not to require one, the design must still be planned, if only mentally. It is an inescapable step to the finished product.

When the design is drawn as a layout, even if simple, one can preview the relationships, and the secondary implications of the design can be seen. This factor alone makes a layout more than useful. The layout also acts as a guide for various contributors and establishes the concept more clearly so that its purpose can be communicated to other

5-3. A layout is a blueprint for the communication to be built.

people. The layout establishes the design, correlates detail, and prevents errors.

Drawing doodles to work out the design concept for yourself is very helpful, and most artists and designers work in this way, producing strange hieroglyphs that serve to define the idea that they are considering. At this stage the doodles are for oneself only as an aid to the process of thought. A designer does not pass these scribblings along but converts them into a more elegant and readable form, meanwhile developing the concept and refining it for presentation.

Almost everyone can doodle his ideas, but it would be a mistake to pass them along to someone else, as he could not possibly bring the same mental images to bear upon them. If you are not a designer but intend to work with a designer, present only the conceptual distillation of your preliminary planning: do not present the doodles. Without refinement no one but you can see your thoughts in them, and they can be a hindrance to what someone else might contribute to the total concept. Make your contribution a thoughtful presentation of the concept and the requirements of the design, something that you know from having studied the design and from your knowledge of the requirements. With the benefit of your concepts and knowledge the designer can contribute his or her expertise to the total design.

These illustrations (5-3, 5-4) are presented primarily to show what a layout is. Though the subject is of no importance for our purposes, in this instance the layouts represent designs for a printed page in a publication: the first is a design for a program cover; the second is a design for reader service in a publication. The designs differ in that the first is formulated conventionally, with the art to be done in the layout design, while the second is formulated from existing art, with the design built around the concept initially presented by the art.

It is important to observe the relative completeness of the layout in its representation of the design. Notice the fact that the design presents the concept for the picture and the relationship between the art and the heading and indicates the copy and how the

5-4. Layouts can be done in a variety of ways. This one is done in pen-and-ink.

communication works. It would be very hard to discern all this information merely by visualizing mentally that the program layout (5-3) is to have type over a picture, with a type panel at the bottom, or that the reader-service layout (5-4) has an illustration at the top, followed by copy and a coupon. The layout expands the concept of a picture image to become a complete design.

The layout is essentially a sketch of how the design is to appear. It can be a layout for the printed page, a series of cards for an audiovisual, a storyboard for a film commercial. The layout may be rendered in any number of media. Pencil is often the preferred medium for a working layout. Ink markers and pens are also very popular: they do not require fixative and do not smudge, making the layout easier to handle. Designer's colors, pastel, and wash are also used to do layouts. Some layouts that must present a very accurate rendition of the finished product actually use photography and some typesetting, but these are more expensive to produce because of the amount of work and material that must go into them.

As a model of the final design the layout must also deal with the environment in which the design will be seen and with its relationship to its surroundings. If practical, the layout is done full-size, because size changes can affect the appearance of the design and what is communicated. If full-size renditions are too difficult or too costly, as is layout for a billboard, for instance, the design is done to scale. For some expensive billboards the design is even presented in a scale model that shows the setting of the display.

One can observe that environmental considerations present many practical details and requirements. As each requirement is considered, it in turn makes its own demands on the design and contributes to shaping the decisions that form the final layout. Along with these practical considerations are considerations of design execution and of costs. These considerations, worked out step-by-step as the design is developed, form a logical process from start to finish. The layout is the visual representation of their development, and because of this the layout is the core of the development and sometimes the only link between the related specialties that will produce the design.

With so much information and work represented by a layout, it is natural to hold perhaps a little too firmly to exactly what is represented. Individuals who deal with the design subsequently often make constructive input, input that serves to modify the design. If these ideas improve the design, they should be used. Yet, strangely, this is often difficult because of the investment in the original layout. To allow flexibility for continued development, it is a good idea to release—mentally—the layout once it is completed. This may sound obvious, but it is sometimes a little harder to do than one might realize. If the design should require further revision, it is nice to be able to pick it up as if you were seeing it for the first time, as if it were somebody else's design.

This idea is often difficult for business-trained people because it may seem illogical. Layouts cost money, but they should be thrown away. The feeling is that, if something does not have a practical use, why is it necessary? Why not proceed directly to the finished product? Yet this thought would not be applied to the manufacture of a product, because everybody knows that to manufacture a product requires that the product be designed and engineered before it can be fabricated. The same thing applies to communication, if in a more abstract sense, and a layout often can save more than its cost in preventing false steps and redos, not to mention the effect that better planning has on quality. The yardstick has to be better communication and the results that it provides.

Sketch and development

Working with professionals has been suggested, but, due to improvements in materials and processes, this is by no means the only way to produce images for communication. Photography, especially with the instant Polaroid and Kodak cameras, can be effective to illustrate an idea. Clip-art services also provide material. Whether working with professionals or on your own, the same stages of development can be used. These stages lead from the idea through the concept used to express the idea to the layout that represents the communication.

The layout objectifies the idea, which is necessary for interaction with others. The graphics display the

concept so that others can react to it. That is why graphics are sometimes called "giraffics"—it's a little like sticking your neck out! If you are working alone, only your own reactions are involved, but if you are working with others or with professionals, their reactions are also involved.

It is quite easy, with the idea in front of you, to see how it can be modified. It is so easy, in fact, that anyone can have an opinion, so it is sometimes wise to limit viewing only to those directly concerned until the idea is sufficiently developed to be viewed critically. If you are working with a professional and if the concept is presented properly, the initial sketch may be a sufficient starting point. If not, contribute what is necessary to the concept and go through the process again.

It should be understood that the people involved in creating a successful communication are working with a purpose. Because of their involvement with the project they are directed less toward criticism and more toward accomplishment. If a number of people are involved, it is important to avoid personal ego trips: your contribution should be relevant to the goal and expressed in terms that others can understand and use. It is also useful to observe that the artist's or designer's contribution, the "giraffics," should not be subject to more criticism than that of the other con-

tributors. It is usually wise to forego criticism when formulating and developing the communication.

Any idea can be developed with sketches and modifications. When one is working for oneself, the initial sketches are very simple, and their development very rapid. If you are working alone, you have all the privileges of artistic temperament, and you will undoubtedly experience this phenomenon: the gap between purpose and accomplishment is uncomfortable. Because the doodles that one does for onself should not be shown, those shown here (5-5) should not be shown either. But for our purposes it is best to illustrate the process that one goes through.

These drawings illustrate some of the doodles that led to the layout of the program cover (5-3). The thinking moved from an initial concept of the picture and copy, to the copy, back to the picture, to a revised version of the initial concept, to a revised picture concept, to more revisions, and "all around Peter's barn," finally arriving at something surprisingly similar to the initial concept. An artist usually thinks in terms of art techniques and of particular picture qualities during this sketch-and-development process. By drawing small the speed of drawing keeps up with the thought, and only the essentials are noted. A sketch is sometimes enlarged to show more detail or to explore certain problems. This

thumbnail sketch (5-6) illustrates this step, and the indication might be clear enough to show someone whom you are working with.

The chicken tracks made during the development of the design concept are a trail of your thoughts, and it is best to be "chicken" about showing them while you are developing the concept, because undue criticism, either your own or that of others, may stymie the flow of thought that provides for development. Each further step in the process can be seen as a new beginning, and one in fact takes this view as the last sketch is discarded in favor of a new and better approach. It is extraordinary how the sketch-and-development process reveals the individual, his or her ideas, hopes, ambitions. These are important qualities for the development of any purpose, and the ideas that the individual presents define the basis of the design. Working first with the basis leads to decisions about particulars. These steps proceed to the objective according to the individual's inspiration.

This development process occurs naturally within the individual, but working alone is not always desirable or possible. In this age of design by committee it is often necessary to incorporate the expertise and knowledge of a number of specialized fields in order to encompass the scope of the project. A most interesting method of doing this is called brainstorm-

5-5. No one would usually see the preliminary design doodles, nor should they be seen. Even another artist would be hard-pressed to see a design in these, yet they are invaluable for developing an idea.

ing, which is a technique in which no criticism is permitted. It recognizes the fact that ideas are presented by the individual. The participants may only present ideas, concepts, perspectives, and interpretations relative to the purpose under discussion. In this greenhouse environment the seedling thought germinates into a concept more quickly than if it had to weather the wintry blasts of self-serving criticism.

The layout sketch proves or disproves the validity of the concept. It retains and coordinates all the detail. It must make concrete what is abstract and reveal any vacuum in rationale, something with which most of us are often plagued when endeavoring to reason through the concept for communication from inception to completion.

In starting with the grand scope of the creative approach we now see that, to deal with the particulars during development, the concept is pruned to fit the reach of our needs and abilities. Even if one asserts that it is not practical to make a creative reach and is preferable to deal with immediate realities, one must also admit that a camera that requires merely

5-6. A more finished thumbnail sketch might be sufficiently readable to show an interested party but not a critical eye.

aiming and the push of a button to produce an immediate illustration allows scarcely any reach at all. It is rather a primitive language that relates most closely to the imagery of thought, requiring little translation from the conceptual process in order to be understood as idea. Even working to the reality of immediacy and practicality allows any individual to present his thoughts and ideas graphically for immediate and practical assimilation by others.

Whether you opt for doing the picture making and designing yourself or for getting help with the project, sketch and development arrive at a representation of the finished communication—a layout. The layout includes the design concept for the picture, the use of copy, and the relationship between the elements. With the idea for the communication in mind the developmental steps formulate the concept using doodles or small sketches as an aid to visualization.

For illustration the abstraction should be particularized in terms of visual imagery. Depending on your own ability or needs, the concept can then be produced in visual form as a sketch by yourself or as a layout executed with the help of a designer or artist. If necessary, the sketch process can be something of a cut-and-try approach, starting with the basic concept and developing the detail and explicitness that is required. The better the initial concept formulation, obviously, the less cutting and trying are required. This, of course, saves money because it saves time and labor. With the art and the copy the layout can be made; the material can now be produced using whatever expertise is needed. If an illustrator or photographer is engaged to do the picture making, a layout prevents a guessing game of trying to interpret a mental concept, which might occur if there were no layout.

It is not unusual for a professional artist or photographer, once he or she can see what you are trying to do, to contribute to, or "plus," your concept. This occurs in the normal order of development and also takes into account the differences in individual idea and interpretation. The layout, which is the end product of sketch and development, is used for coordination and communication, while the finished art, the pictures and copy, is the final public presentation.

As the initiator you are the judge of how much

development is needed and of how refined the picture communication should be. Your own knowledge of needs and conditions will indicate what is appropriate. Many communication needs do not have to be so developed as to require professional help, and simply produced photography can save much written explanation and description.

This process is used to produce illustration and communication from scratch, but there are few situations in which there is no existing material, few situations in which the communication cannot be developed using material at hand or readily available. In order to use existing material, the approach to design is somewhat different. One has to fit the concept to the existing material to express the idea to be communicated. The process of concept formulation is similar to working from scratch, but at first it can seem a bit like working backwards.

Working backwards

Working backwards is required when the art exists before the concept. The term refers to the procedure by which the design concept is reached. It is like hitching the cart to the horse instead of the horse to the cart. The results are exactly the same—only the approach is different, as it must be to make use of existing art.

Working backwards also starts with the initial idea for the communication. The difference in formulation begins with the concept development of the visual image. Instead of looking at our own imagery we look at what is available in the existing art to express the idea—this is the working-backwards part. Instead of fitting the image to the concept we fit the concept to the existing image and make the concept express the idea for the communication. This is why what we want to say must be very clear in our thought.

This method is not so unusual as it might seem at first. For example, when we express ourselves with language, we may choose from any number of similar words the one closest to our idea: the same procedure occurs with existing picture images selected from the shelf of availability. As the word expresses the concept used to communicate our idea, so the existing picture expresses the concept used to communicate our idea. We should expand our "vocabulary" of picture availability in order to have a selection of graphic possibilities.

Graphic possibilities are extensive in most instances, although often unrecognized. Consider business or company literature, which is available without copyright, for a start. It would include letterheads, logos, emblems, advertising, packaging, publicity photos, and similar material. Shop or working drawings, especially isometric drawings, can be photographically reduced in size and cleaned up by eliminating extraneous technical notations. Clip-art services offer a great selection of art that can be purchased inexpensively, and publications such as newspapers often offer to their advertisers the use of several clip-art services. The larger newspapers may have extensive libraries of clip art. Add to this the simple art that anyone might prepare: artist's aids, such as transfer type and pictures; simple diagrams and charts; simple photography of business facilities, trucks, and signs: the possibilities are numerous and varied. If you are working within a much smaller organization, consider using only a clip-art service, which is available to all because of its nominal cost.

The importance of a clear view of the objective before starting the process cannot be overstressed. With it clearly established one looks for the pieces that build up to it. Holding the objective in view, one goes through the available material. At this point one might think that using clip art or existing art is not a creative process. This is not true, because the connecting concept must be supplied, and it calls for creativity of thought or at least clever innovation. From necessity one must confront a new application. Because the new application requires a concept, users of existing art often start with two strikes against them: they believe—strike one—that just clipping a picture doesn't require any thinking and that—strike two—they can find a picture of what they are talking about.

One may start with the subject matter to be communicated, but, depending on the subject, the possibilities may be quickly exhausted. This is strike three, the point at which many people throw up their hands. But if one is looking for specific subject matter in a random environment that is not organized as a card file in a library is, one may reasonably expect that it would be unlikely to chance upon a picture of the subject. Again, checking for pictures that logically imply or reasonably associate to the subject may be unfruitful, because one must have organization to locate the idea, once it is conceived. Unless one has access to a highly organized clip file, this will prove impossible.

The larger clip-art services are highly organized, with art on any number of subjects; but, when faced with limited classification or organization, it is easier to simply go through what is most promising and to let the art that you are handling suggest possibilities. As you handle the art, it will suggest through association concepts that relate to the communication that you are working with. This is an active, not a theoretical, practice. The most unlikely art sometimes works beautifully if you make the right conceptual

5-7. The sequence of steps for working backwards with existing art shows how the pen-and-ink layout (5-4) was related and developed.

connection. A technique, a face, a gesture, clothing, environment, or whatever else may catch your eye can make the necessary connection for the communication that you wish to make. Because of its unpredictability and subtlety this process works better in a spontaneous format.

The drawing used in the winter layout (5-4) makes the connection because it seems appropriate in character. It suggests the winter theme, and the word "winter" can also be clipped. From this point it is simply a matter of working out the copy and layout of the design. The sequence of steps is illustrated here (5-7). Again, the layout determines whether or not the concept works. This paste-up (5-8) shows the art positioned and indicates the source.

One may consider art selection as a process of discovery: one selects the most desirable art from the shelf, discovers the concept, and adapts the concept and the copy to make use of the art. The process can be creative if it is allowed to be; it can suggest new approaches and even contribute to the objective if one is open to this possibility. Some clip-art serv-

KING COMMUNICATIONS CORP.
1234 Kings Road, Los Angeles, CA 90000

SHOPPER'S INFORMATION SERVICE

...OUR ADVERTISERS HELP YOU TO GET READY
With winter ahead, now is the time to get ready. The goods and services advertised here let you shop for the best buys. And NOW is the time, before the temperature drops. We make every effort to accept only those advertisements that present legitimate value, and the advertisers appreciate your continued patronage.

1. DEVELOP CONCEPT

2. PICK UP EXISTING ART

CLIP ART

CLIP ART

LOGO & EMBLEM

KING COMMUNICATIONS CORP.
1234 Kings Road, Los Angeles, CA 90000

SHOPPER'S
INFORMATION
SERVICE

---

3. DEVELOP CONCEPT WITH COPY

4. PROVE DESIGN

5. TYPESET COPY

COPY

LAYOUT

TYPESET

TITLE SHOPPER'S SERVICE AD -- 2 col x 10   PAGE NO. 1 of 1

COUNT |1 2 3 4 5 6 7 8 9 10|1 2 3 4 5 6 7 8 9 20|1 2 3 4 5 6 7 8 9 30|1 2 3 4 5 6 7 8 9 40|1 2 3 4 5 6 7 8 9 50|

1 (Shopper's Service Emblem and Illustration)

2 Winter

3 ...OUR ADVERTISERS HELP YOU TO GET READY

4

5 With winter ahead, now is the time to get ready. The goods

6 and services advertised here let you shop for the best buys.

7 And NOW is the time, before the temperature drops. We make

8 every effort to accept only those advertisements that

9 present legitimate value, and the advertisers appreciate

10 your continued patronage.

11 Shopper's Information Service: For more information on any

12 product or service, circle the ad number (found at the bottom

13 of each advertisement) on the coupon below, and send it to us.

14 We take it from there.

15

16 (LOGO in Coupon)

17

18 Circle Advertisement Number and check Item wanted:

19 1   2   3   4   5   6   7   8   9 10 11 12 13 14 15

20 16 17 18 19 20 21 22 23 24 25 26 27 28 29 30

21 __ Please have a salesman call

22 __ Send additional information

23 __ Send catalog

24 Name   Address   City   State   Zip Code

...OUR ADVERTISERS HELP YOU TO GET READY

With winter ahead, now is the time to get ready. The goods and services advertised here let you shop for the best buys. And NOW is the time, before the temperature drops. We make every effort to accept only those advertisements that present legitimate value, and the advertisers appreciate your continued patronage.

Shopper's Information Service: For more information on any product or service, circle the ad number (found at the bottom of each advertisement) on the coupon below, and send it to us. We take it from there.

Circle Advertisement Number and check Item wanted:

1   2   3   4   5   6   7   8   9   10   11   12   13   14   15
16   17   18   19   20   21   22   23   24   25   26   27   28   29   30

☐ Please have a salesman call
☐ Send additional information
☐ Send catalog

FIND CLIP ART

PICK UP EMBLEM

CLIP ART HEADING

SHOPPER'S
INFORMATION
SERVICE

Winter

...OUR ADVERTISERS HELP YOU TO GET READY

With winter ahead, now is the time to get ready. The goods and services advertised here let you shop for the best buys. And NOW is the time, before the temperature drops. We make every effort to accept only those advertisements that present legitimate value, and the advertisers appreciate your continued patronage.

Shopper's Information Service: For more information on any product or service, circle the ad number (found at the bottom of each advertisement) on the coupon below, and send it to us. We take it from there.

TYPESET COPY

PICK UP LOGO

KING COMMUNICATIONS CORP.
1234 Kings Road, Los Angeles, CA 90000

Circle Advertisement Number and check Item wanted:

1	2	3	4	5	6	7	8	9	10	11	12	13	14	15
16	17	18	19	20	21	22	23	24	25	26	27	28	29	30

☐ Please have a salesman call

☐ Send additional information

☐ Send catalog

NAME

ADDRESS

CITY   STATE   ZIP CODE

PASTE-UP COUPON

ices, which provide very good art and concept starters, may even spur you to improve your presentation by suggesting alternatives to the concept that you would have chosen if you had been left to your own devices.

If the development of art from scratch is thought of as building from the concept to the communication, working backwards might be thought of as hunting for the concept to the communication. In the end result both are logical presentations, but finding the image concept, which is the key to the communication, is more easily handled when working backwards from free association with the art. The logic of inference can be employed only in relation to the particular picture being handled. In a situation that provides a comprehensive catalog of subject matter applying too much logic beforehand in pursuit of an unknown concept only serves to block out other possibilities: one's approach can become too rigid if one brings preconceived notions to the search for the concept.

To be clear about the subject and about what needs to be said does not and, especially in the case of clip art, should not imply a crystallized concept on the way in which the communication will be said. Without flexibility in means one may find the use of clip art very frustrating indeed, because it is scarcely possible that any service, no matter how comprehensive, well organized and cataloged, can provide for all possible needs. The situation appears even more limited if one is working with business material. Yet the clever innovator can come up with a fresh way of using the material. Looking at the material with an eye to its relation to your subject is the way to find new concepts.

With the art in hand, the copy is written to the concept suggested by the art; the layout is designed; and the material is produced as before. With the working-backwards method the copy is almost always written to the art; by comparison, when working without existing art, the copy is often written first. Working backwards requires that the art produce the concept or means for communication; working without existing art requires the concept to produce the art.

5-8. When the concept is developed and the material produced and assembled, the ad is put together as a paste-up. This reduced version of the paste-up shows the origin of each element.

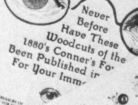

6. CLIP ART

Clip art is one of the more important resources of existing art. This is so simply because of its sheer volume and availability. Given its volume, there should always be something useful, even to one with limited experience or ability in inventing concepts for the use of the art.

The term "clip art" refers primarily to art that can be clipped and used as material in a paste-up prepared for offset printing. The art can also be used with other forms of reproduction. The word "clip" may have unpleasant connotations, but it means anything that is scissored or cut—clipped—from printed material designed for reuse. Clip art is prepared by an art service specifically for the purpose of reuse in a particular application, and the material is printed on one side only, using paper of a quality suitable for proof reproduction and mounting in a paste-up. The collection of art material is normally bound as a book or magazine for convenience of handling. The photo (6-1) shows a number of books offered by clip-art services.

6-1. Clip-art books are offered by a number of producers. Some are one-time presentations; others are continuing services. The Stamps Conhaim book at the bottom of the pile is a full newspaper-sheet size.

The predecessor of the clip art now in general use for paste-up and offset printing was the newspaper mat service. The newspaper mat service supplied the art, reproduced in a catalog, and the mats to cast a plate of the art for use with letterpress printing. The difference is one of degree in that offset printing does not require a raised-surface printing plate and allows more freedom in the use of the art for paste-up. With increased use of offset printing, which requires only the image, the art service need only supply clip-art books. Clip art also has a wider application with the more general use of offset printing and its application to business use.

Since the production of clip art is an art or an advertising service, books of clip art are often offered on a periodic or monthly subscription basis. The subscribers are those with a continuing need for reproduction art, such as advertisers, newspapers, and printers. With the wider use of clip art, books are also presented for one-time purchase. These books of clip art are available at art-supply stores, from some large stationery suppliers, and directly by mail order from producers.

Suppliers are sometimes large art services that have been in business a long time and that employ a number of artists, while others are groups of several

6-2. These ten books, produced by the Volk Art Studio, contain well over a hundred illustrations, yet all could be obtained for less than the cost of producing a single piece of artwork. The dimensions are approximately 8 x 5 inches, half the size of a sheet of notepaper.

commercial studio artists who sporadically produce a clip book. Two large suppliers that offer high-quality art and that have been in business over the years are Stamps Conhaim (SCW, Inc., 20433 Nordhoff, Chatsworth, CA 91311), which was originally a newspaper-advertising mat service; and the Volk Art Studio (Volk Corp., Pleasantville, N.J. 08232), which is aimed more to advertisers and in-house art services. The Stamps Conhaim service is sold by subscription in two different sizes and is available to advertisers using the subscribing newspaper. The

Volk Art Service is available by subscription and also in library sets packaged for one-time purchase, some of which cost less than a single small drawing.

The price of clip art is so low that in some cases the use of a single illustration justifies the cost of the whole package; the use of more than one illustration brings the cost far under what would be necessary to produce the art for one illustration. The fact that high-quality books of clip art may be purchased so inexpensively also makes clip art a resource that anyone can afford as an individual purchase and enhances its availability. These books (6-2) can be obtained for less than the cost of a small illustration, a spot drawing. As a buyer of the services of a newspaper, printer, or business that subscribes one has the use of the art "free," and you can't "clip" art better than that.

As an aid to utilizing clip art one should realize that the supply is geared to one of several markets. Basic to the clip-art market is the newspaper: a number of services are available to newspapers. Other services are aimed at a more general advertising market and are prepared with circulars, brochures, and direct mail in mind. Again, there are collections of clip art prepared for very broad usage in terms of subject but designed specifically for general job printing, including stationery, business cards, forms, flyers, and a host of other items for small business.

An awareness of the purpose of the clip-art package aids in understanding its organization. For instance, a newspaper service is likely to be organized into a chronology of events around which sales promotions are built: there are promotional events for every month from New Year's Eve to Christmas. There are also innovations and advertising devices. If you were looking for hearts and flowers, for example, you could start with St. Valentine's Day in February and look through Spring, Easter, and June weddings. Hard-lines merchandise would be most easily located in summer-fix-up months or after-Christmas sales. In a similar manner a general advertising service might follow retail and industrial advertising specialities, with subject matter cataloged by event or activity. But there is nothing to prevent switching the use of the art: the criterion, after all, is the way in which the art is used.

It is true that the art is not crafted and individualized to a specific application, but in many cases in which the cost of specific art is not justified the use of clip art or existing art is the best choice. To phrase it in the vernacular of mass merchandising, if you can't afford the custom-made one-of-a-kind, you can afford the mass-produced product and customize it with a selection of options.

The options available for use of clip art or any existing art, beyond the application of one's own concepts, are size changes, additions, deletions, and picture combinations. Changing the size alters the texture and the appearance of the technique; additions can individualize the art; deletions can change the context and the character; combining foregrounds and backgrounds can change the setting.

Implicit in the preparation of art offered by a clip-art service is a consideration of its possible final uses. The clip-art service can present ideas to the user in this regard. What may be more subtle to the observer is the application of concept implicit in the art, such as the picture concept of an American family or a concept of a business or service as it is used to produce the art. This relates to the size and technique used for the art and to the general tone of interpretation used in handling its subject.

While these concepts can sometimes seem quite limiting if they are inappropriate to the intended use, they can be easily altered to suit the concept of the user: that is, the user can superimpose his concept on that of the art through the use that he makes of it. The user has the last word.

A more difficult level of inappropriateness to deal with is the obvious necessity for clip art to be nonspecific in order to be suitable to the greatest number of users. The specific concept of the user can usually compensate for this with copy and through the relationship of the art to the content or the concept of its use. Until the art is seen in the context of its intended use, it is merely raw material, as are words in a dictionary, which must be placed in the context of a sentence to provide meaning and nuance of connotation.

The greater one's skill in adapting the art, the easier it is to use clip art. The application of one's own concept for the communication, the adaptation and editing of the art, and the understanding of the organization of the clip-art file in order to obtain a selection of art all enter into the use of clip art as a resource of existing art.

Existing art

Existing art is anything that can be used for illustrative purposes that exists prior to the need for the art. Existing art is perhaps a better term than clip art, though clip art is the term in common usage. Although the term "clip art" is often applied to anything that can be reused, it is used in a more particular sense here to refer to art prepared specifically for reuse; "existing art" is an all-inclusive term that covers anything that can conceivably be reused for illustration. It would include anything in graphic form in the way of pictures or drawings, advertising and promotional material, packaging and signs, and development, manufacturing, and design material. It would even include materials that could be turned to graphic use through reproduction photography, such as emblems or products similar to bas-relief art, which present a graphic surface and which can be used as art copy on a reproduction camera. Existing art includes all resources of clip art, transfer art, and graphic material out of copyright.

Copyrighted material, of course, cannot be used without the originator's permission. This fact should be stressed, and every user of graphic material should respect the property rights of others, as he would want his own respected. All art produced and sold as clip art is copyrighted: the right to use it is conferred upon payment for the package. Use without payment or right of use is therefore comparable to stealing a publication or product that belongs to somebody else. Because the art is sometimes altered and one step removed in use through reproduction, this fact does not always seem clear to everyone. There are also other rights of use pertaining to identity, public image, and business goodwill that can be infringed, and these are more difficult and expensive to correct than a mere restoration of payment for a one-time use of copyrighted art.

Copyright law in some applications can be very complex, far more so than that pertaining to the example of the use of clip art. While the copyright

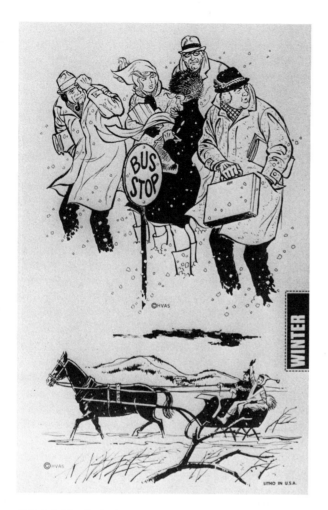

6-3, 6-4. The illustration on the top back cover of a Volk Studio clip-art book was used for this example. The adaptation at the far right shows how flexible clip art can be. The bottom figure was clipped and the snow eliminated to show a cold, windy day, eliminating the need for any drawing. The hypothetical ad for a transit company was developed around the bus-stop sign.

law does not allow any unauthorized use of copyrighted material, court interpretations permit what is called "fair use." This is vaguely interpreted as the use of a small part of the whole when it does not harm the copyright owner. It is under this interpretation of the fair-use doctrine that critics and scholars use small portions of copyrighted material. In recent years this interpretation has been broadened due to the development of reprographics, and one finds copying machines in public libraries for the convenience of the public. The copiers make actual reproductions and of more than a small part, but it is assumed that these copies are for personal or private use. The next step in the sequence of development is the reproduction of the copy for the use of "friends" of the copyist. This is a common practice with everything from cartoons to musical scores. When does this become harmful to the copyright owner? In the case of some newsletter publishers it threatens to put them out of business; in the case of other publishers it may actually serve as a boost due to the publicity.

There are thus clear instances when one must make a decision as to what constitutes "fair use," whether or not this use is intentioned, and whether the adaptation could be harmful to the originator. If there is any doubt, it is wise to ask for permission to use the material, because some copyright owners are of necessity extremely strict in their interpretation of "fair use," and the attorneys of these owners may do more than suggest that you cease to use their material. It is to be recommended that this policy by adhered to even if copyright (©) is not indicated, because the same legalities apply to claim of ownership.

Although the question of copyright has been dwelt on at some length, it does not limit the user of existing art. It merely points to the use of existing art that is copyright-free, art that is available. Art that is copyrighted is merely not available; and, since it is in use by someone else, it would be a bad choice anyway, as your graphic identity might be confused in the public mind with that of someone else.

The question of graphic identity, which arises with repeated use of a characteristic symbol or design in public presentation, can be raised about the use of clip art in general. The question is: if one uses clip art to build a graphic identity, what is to prevent someone else from buying and using the same clip art? The answer is: nothing, although the possibility of such a coincidence is remote. One has to think of this question in relation to a local or regional market, because it is unlikely that clip art would be used if there were a budget for extensive or national promotion. In the case of a newspaper advertising service, in which such a similarity of display could be compared, the service prevents this possibility by offering only one of each piece of art: when it is clipped and used, it isn't there for someone else to use. Some services do present several sizes of the same art: you should check for this possibility and clip all sizes if duplication would hurt your advertising. Size changes and different applications usually so change the overall appearance that illustration identity is not a significant factor. If advertisers found graphic identity that much of a problem, none of them would use the word "New!"

An example of exercising one's options to edit existing art to suit will clarify the individualizing effects of the application. Clip art is used in the example because of its availability and its freedom from copyright restrictions. To indicate that this applies in some degree to any existing art, the example can be made with any clip art: the top back cover of a Volk Studio clip-art book first presented itself and is used here (6-3).

The doublethink involved in preparing clip art is shown in our example which individualizes the art. In order to show the individualization process, the entire application to the final use must also be brought into the example. The example thus shows the individualizing process, its effect when clip art is applied to a specific use, and an example of the application of clip art to a specific use. It shows how any illustration may be individualized by editing, and it does so in the context of a hypothetical application. Reasoning the development of our example on these pages is as much a use of clip art as is its final application in a hypothetical advertisement.

To develop a subject from the illustration as it is applied in the example, we see that, because of the bus-stop sign, it suggests a transit company. This is a logical choice, because transit companies have limited advertising budgets yet need a variety of printed material, ranging from schedules to posters, and can conceivably make good use of clip art. Let us assume that the bus-stop sign is accurate and that the illustration does appeal to the transit company for this reason. (If the bus-stop sign were not accurate, the use of the illustration for this subject would not be valid, unless this detail were changed or omitted.) To further adapt the illustration to a

6-5. Letraset clip art is presented on transparent carrier sheets. The sample shown above at actual size was taken from the lower-right-hand corner of the 10-x-15-inch sheet at left.

specific situation, let us assume that the city location has cold weather but usually not much snow. The application of our example will be a half-page advertisement to appear in a theater program, something useful but necessarily budget-conscious because of its limited circulation. In the context of the subject chosen for the example the objective is to produce a successful half-page ad for the transit company.

The half-page space can be made up of one of two possible configurations, a horizontal half or a vertical half. The somewhat horizontal bias and the directional view of the turned heads in the illustration indicate a horizontal space, but a vertical space is to be preferred in this application, because a half-page ad in a program can be placed below another ad. The dark figure in the center of the illustration faces back into the ad. If the other figures were edited out of the composition, the central figure alone would still carry the idea; it is also possible to eliminate the snow from the composition, because it is line art and the blowing muffler and coat and the attitude of the figure also indicate coldness. The illustration would have more verticality if the other figures were taken out, and it could be enlarged and used in a vertical space.

Eliminating so much of the original illustration is a more extreme use of one's options. It is accomplished very simply in the paste-up by carefully cutting around the portion of the illustration to be used. Eliminating the snow requires cutting away or

whiting out the indication of snowflakes and blacking in the pattern that they make against the dark coat. This, of course, leaves the drawing incomplete, because in the original the feet are buried in the snowfall: this can be handled by cropping at the lower leg or by placing something in the foreground over the missing portion of the drawing. In this case a logo panel can both cover and crop the illustration.

The idea to be presented is dependability, and the copy is limited to the heading "You can depend on us . . ." (6-4). It should be obvious, however, that any number of sales and copy ideas could be related to the illustration. The transit-company use works because of the illustration's initial appeal. It originated the process of developing the concept for the advertisement.

The first picture to come to hand was chosen, not because it represents an ultimate in clip art, though it is a good clip-art illustration, but because it shows that nearly every illustration has enough content to initiate a conceptual process. By exercising the options of editing, altering the setting, and changing the size the illustration can be adapted to the purpose. The example indicates the extent to which this can be done. The hypothetical situation is contrived for this purpose, but the possibility exists with any illustration to be used as existing art.

The example approaches the clip art—existing art—as raw material to be shaped to the purpose,

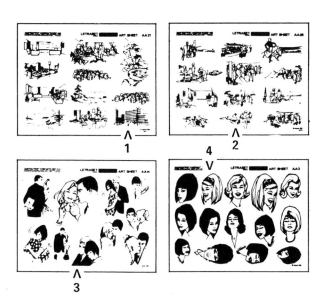

6-6. Four separate pieces of art are composed into a single illustration. The design of Letraset's Art Sheets permits any number of illustrations to be combined. You can select from sheets of heads; hands; half and full figures of men, women, and children; and backgrounds. One need only compose the elements: no drawing ability is required.

and it indicates the ease with which illustration can be used conceptually to communicate an idea. Consider how quickly the picture idea can be taken in compared to the written explanation. Both are necessary here because they fulfill different functions: the written rationale might not have been immediately obvious simply from making the comparison between the original clip-art illustration and its use in an application.

Transfer art

Transfer art is mounted on a carrier sheet in the same manner as is transfer type. It can be used in much the same way as can clip art, but, because it is presented as an image on a carrier sheet and marketed as transfer type, it has certain distinguishing features. The most obvious difference is perhaps that a single sheet of transfer art can be bought at a time. Transfer art has wide distribution in that it is sold along with transfer type at art-materials stores and stationery stores and costs only a few dollars a sheet. This fact should make transfer art the most available and least expensive source of existing art.

Producers of transfer art vary in terms of the amount and quality of art offered: some catalog only a few sheets of figures, cars, and items primarily designed for use on architectural drawings, while other manufacturers offer a more extensive catalog.

Letraset, one of the major manufacturers and distributors of transfer products (Letraset USA, Inc., 33 New Bridge Road, Bergenfield, N.J. 07621), has a very extensive selection of Art Sheets.

The photo (6-5) shows two sheets offered by Letraset; more are displayed in miniature in their catalog. Notice the stylized character of the art as compared to clip art and the consistent style. This allows different pieces of art to be combined in one illustration. The sheets are arranged by subject to facilitate combination. The sheets include heads; hands; half and full figures of men, women, and children; and backgrounds. The quality of art is evident from the example, and it is carefully designed with respect to the needs of the user so that, due to the nature of the stylization, most can adapt the package to their needs.

While the amount of art available on transfer sheets can hardly be compared to what is available as clip art, transfer art meets the requirement of versatility by the ease with which various pieces of art or portions of illustrations may be combined. It is a simple matter to transfer a portion of a drawing or to remove unwanted parts of a transferred drawing.

Transfer art differs from clip art, which is handled as pieces of paper, in that the transferred image may be scraped off or erased before it is tightly burnished down. Corrections, white paint, or edges of paper do not show in reproductions, but transfer art presents a more finished appearance for original art used for display, as a flip chart.

This feature of transfer art—that only the image transfers—offers advantages in other applications as well. The spaces in and around the lines are open, making transfer art suitable for use on transparent material such as acetate: it can be placed on cells to be used over background art, for example, or on transparencies for overhead projection. While any art can be made into film for projection, transfer art may be used directly.

This feature is also useful when illustration is combined with type or another form of art and when the lines overlap, because it allows the art to be prepared directly for use with duplicating equipment, which can handle only one image. More sophisticated reproduction techniques, by comparison, can reproduce any number of levels of art by means of overprinting different negatives. Transfer art provides the direct and economical solution to this requirement by eliminating the need for overlays.

In its simplest applications transfer art might be easier for the novice to manipulate than clip art. While clipping and paste-up are simple, nothing is easier and quicker than to rub a transfer image onto a sheet of paper by running a ballpoint pen lightly over it until it releases onto the paper beneath. If the placement of the art is in doubt, the transfer image can be placed on a separate sheet of paper and assembled into a paste-up. Once transferred, the art is burnished down and it cannot be moved: if it is necessary to change the position of the art, it must be removed and a new image transferred at the new location.

Combining images of transfer art can become more complicated, but it certainly requires no drawing ability. It primarily requires a sense of composition, as does the use and placement of any art. The simplest combination of transfer art is to place a background with a foreground. The background is the environment, and the foreground is the subject. The background and foreground art can actually be placed side by side, which is often easier than overlapping the art. Whereas clip art is usually more detailed and can require editing to suit the application, transfer art may be adapted to the application by adding detail.

This example combines four different pieces of art (6-6). The background of the building is transferred first; the sportscar and group of figures are placed in front of the building scene in what will become the middle distance; the couple is placed in the middle foreground; and the head of the girl is placed in the near foreground. As long as the scale of each succeeding drawing is larger, this can be arranged, and the art sheets are designed to provide approximately four different scales of art. The background scenes are, of course, the smallest in scale.

In the example the smallest scale is at the left, the largest at the right. The common denominator of all four scenes is the level of the horizon. As long as the horizon is consistent, the subjects and figures may be shifted to stage left or stage right for the best compositional effect. The composition in the example produces a strong left-to-right sense of movement, which is balanced to some extent by the prominent black of the man's suit and the woman's hair in the center of the picture. The four pieces of art overlap slightly, which tends to unify the composition. It also requires that some of the transferred art be removed so as to not show through the line art placed on top.

Combining art is not as difficult as it might seem, because the art is on a transparent carrier sheet, and the art underneath can be seen before the overlapping art is transferred. The transparency allows different arrangements to be tried before determining the final composition and burnishing the art down.

The Letraset Art Sheets are a system of illustration. Their use requires no drawing, and they can be combined in many ways. The versatility of the 500-plus illustrations is greatly enhanced by the way in which they are designed. They may be used as simple spot drawings, as they appear on the carrier sheets, and, because of the consistent style, the relatively constant placement of the horizon, and the relatively consistent scale of four sizes, they can also be composed into atmospheric or storytelling illustrations to enhance the communication of an idea.

If there are objections to the possible similarity of art style to that of another user, it may be answered that style is well designed to suit its purpose, not to call attention to itself, and to fit almost any kind of application to a subject. Transfer art, with its advantage of a transparent carrier sheet, is really designed for application to situations in which comparisons of style would not be appropriate, such as in-house publications, circulars, direct mail, promotional pieces, displays, presentations, and slides, application in which the material stands alone. There are also applications in which the convenience and nominal expense of several Art Sheets make the use of transfer art very appropriate.

Quaint cuts and sorts

"Quaint" is a term applied to art that pleasingly suggests customs of former generations. Quaint cuts and sorts are copyright-free illustrations and symbols on which the copyright has expired. They can be used as a source of art and clipped by anyone.

"Cut" is a term for a block or engraving used in letterpress printing to reproduce art and thus became synonymous with art. Quaint cuts are antiques; they are usually line art, which makes them easy to reproduce; they are wood cuts and steel engravings taken from the printer. In some cases they are taken from materials that have become obsolete. Others may have been drawn from the printer's devil box, a box in which unused printing materials were thrown and in which they have stood forgotten for long years in a dusty corner. Collectors go through old materials sold at auctions and in estates for such wonderful finds.

While quaint cuts are antique illustrations, sorts are smaller, more symbolic or stylized pictures, which are combined with typesetting. A sort is a character in a font of type. Because sorts are stylized, they sometimes seem strangely up to date, but more often they have an antique quality, either

6-7. This is a small sampling of the many quaint cuts and sorts available as an illustration source to the ingenious user of existing art. This art is used in special circumstances because of its antique flavor. Some of the more stylized illustrations lend themselves to use as design motifs.

QUAINT CUTS

TYPOGRAPHIC SORTS

because of the line-art technique or because the picture is illustrated from a point of view that is no longer fashionable.

Many pieces of this type of art are assembled into collections, which are published in book form for clipping and reuse. The reproduction (6-7) shows a brief sampling of the character of quaint cuts and sorts. Notice particularly the sort of the abstract phone. Books of collections are available in art stores and in some bookstores. Two publishers of note are the Art Direction Book Company (Art Direction Book Co., 19 West 44th Street, New York, N.Y. 10036) and The Dick Sutphen Studio (The Dick Sutphen Studio, Box 628, Scottsdale, Arizona 85252). The character of each collection differs. Some may focus on memorabilia, others on figures, still others on historic scenes. The use of such art must take into account its quality and its age, but there are as many possibilities as one has the imagination to invent.

Quaint cuts and sorts, needless to say, are nostalgic. They can be used to create a different atmosphere for a business message. It is usually richly decorative and ornamental, in keeping with the art. The ornamental quality can be striking, especially because the style of the art is so out of context with the norm. Quaint art and sorts play upon fashion because of their antiquity. What seems eccentric and humorous can also be charming if used in this way. Humor is difficult to use for communication, but it can be very effective if the art and the copy strike the right balance.

Because the collections are organized by theme, uses are often suggested, but one is not limited to these ideas. Animal subjects, for instance, may suggest a different treatment, because, although drawn in an antique style, they always have the same shape and form—they are never out of date.

The size of an illustration can determine its use. The normally smaller size of this art lends itself to atmospheric and decorative use. This is a style of design in which the art is used to support the message, which is primarily communicated by written copy and typesetting. This design style illustrates the use of spot art as opposed to feature illustration. In using spot art the art stylizes and ornaments the message and is used for decoration instead of directly conveying the message. Its function is to create an atmosphere or a frame of reference for interpreting the message.

This layout (6-8) is a typical example of this kind of design, though an endless number of variations are possible. The various elements used, such as ornamentation and cartouche, are typical of this style. The main characteristics of the art are its supportive quality and the fact that the message is communicated with type display.

This design can be used with any style of art. It is not a pure period design because of its asymmetrical balance: a true period design would probably be symmetrical. The fact that the design can be so readily adapted is indicative of the possibilities available with this art. As photography became more dominant after World War II, spot drawing began to be used less extensively; with the revival of interest in spot drawings and atmospheric art they should again become popular.

This kind of design is particularly suited to quaint cuts and sorts because of their necessarily non-specific use. It is unlikely that one would find a specific picture of a particular item or situation: the art can convey only the atmosphere that works with the message. The message must be in words, in signs that spell out the idea. Because of the difficulty and expense of producing woodcuts most art from this period was small, and the message was conveyed with ornate typography. That the same style is again popular today, although in different terms and with different reproduction techniques, allows the effective reuse of this material.

Because the "old" is becoming more valuable and because the trend is to appreciate a new value in our history, quaint cuts and sorts should receive more attention and find greater use. The newer technology of offset printing, while different in character and quality than letterpress printing, makes possible the use of antique art in new ways. Quaint cuts and sorts are an interesting and high-quality resource of existing art that combines well with the many new and sometimes eccentric typeface designs now available in transfer type and photolettering designs.

6-8. This layout sketch with callouts serves as a schematic guide for the use of quaint cuts and sorts. Humor and special circumstances extend the possibilities.

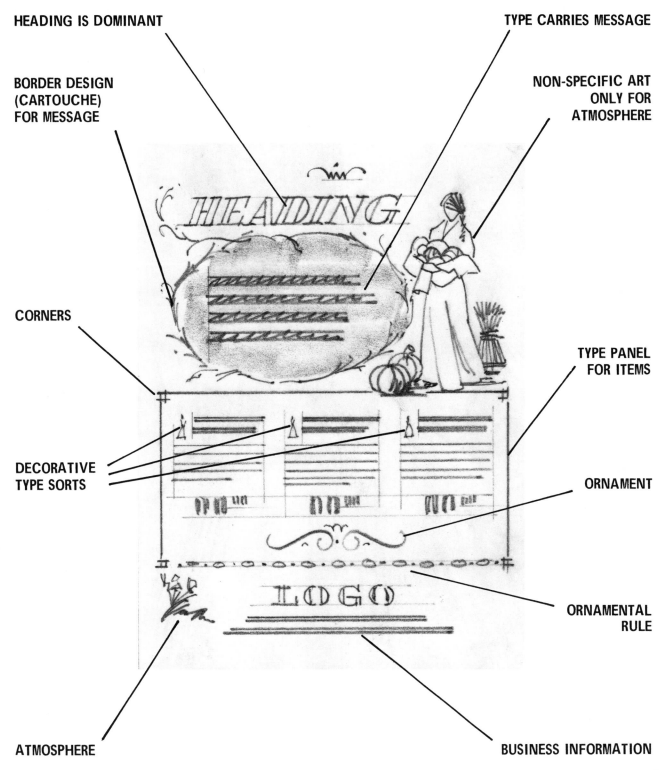

HEADING IS DOMINANT

TYPE CARRIES MESSAGE

BORDER DESIGN
(CARTOUCHE)
FOR MESSAGE

NON-SPECIFIC ART
ONLY FOR
ATMOSPHERE

CORNERS

TYPE PANEL
FOR ITEMS

DECORATIVE
TYPE SORTS

ORNAMENT

ORNAMENTAL
RULE

ATMOSPHERE

BUSINESS INFORMATION

7. PHOTOGRAPHY

Photography is the most popular picture resource. If you speak of making a picture, most people will assume that you mean taking a snapshot. Because we are so accustomed to taking pictures, because we see and use so many photographs, because the technology of photography is so highly developed, it seems easiest to grab a camera if an illustration is needed.

Most of us have some kind of camera; a simple camera is not expensive and provides the means to make a picture. Yet, for all its availability, a photo is not always automatically the easiest method of illustrating an idea. One must remember that a photo is continuous-tone and that for print reproduction or duplication it must be made into a halftone. There is also the need to process the film and to print the picture—only the Polaroid and Kodak instant camera provide a picture immediately, which is a great convenience in many applications. In fact, a special adaptation of the Land Polaroid Camera can make pictures with a halftone screen. Though the Polaroid

cameras cannot substitute for all other cameras in every application, within the 4-x-5-inch format it has many applications. The Polaroid MP-3 Land camera can be used very conveniently for quick photocopies. One film, the type-51 4-x-5-inch Land film, is a high-contrast material designed specifically for graphic-art use: it produces an opaque-paper print in which tones are rendered as almost pure blacks and whites.

There have been many and continuous improvements in the technology of photography: better film, price reductions, and reasonably priced cameras that produce an instant picture. The photo (7-1) indicates a 50-year span of camera, from the early Eastman Kodak camera of the 1920s (shown at the top), to the development of the Land Polaroid Camera during the 1950s (center), to the Yashicamat twin-lens-reflex camera of the 1960s (bottom), to the single-lens-reflex (SLR) popular today (not shown).

The Eastman Kodak camera shown in this illustration required an enormous amount of light to make pictures, due to its small lens and slow film, compared to the SLR and fast fine-grained film available today. This model has a 7.7 lens and uses 3¼-x-4¼-inch film; the Yashicamat has a 3.5 lens and uses 2¼-x-2¼-inch film; the SLR popular today has a 1.2.

7-1. From top to bottom three cameras are shown in the sequence of their development. The Polaroid camera at left and the twin-lens reflex at right are still popular, the first because of its instant pictures and the second because of the size of the film.

7-2. A suitable background helps to define the subject of the picture. In this example a particular leaf is the subject: this is understood and seen when the subject is isolated, as on the right.

1.4, or a 1.8 lens, with other lenses available, and uses 35mm film. Lenses have become larger and less expensive, film smaller and faster, and cameras lighter and more compact. The H.R. Land Polaroid Camera shown in the illustration is the 80A, an early model; beautifully made, it proved the workability of and popularized instant photography. Today's Polaroid cameras are easier to use and much less expensive, and they take bigger pictures.

In 50 years there have been many changes in the technology of photography. The last 25 years have seen even more rapid improvements, with many new manufacturers entering the field. The Japanese manufacturers made large lenses economical and fine cameras less expensive; faster and finer film popularized the 35mm camera and made it suitable for a great variety of photographic work; today's instant-picture cameras are popularly priced and simple to use—just aim and shoot.

These continued developments extend the capabilities of camerawork. With a camera you don't need to know how to draw. The camera is truly a popular tool for making a picture, and experienced photographers with fine cameras and equipment can do more than just "snap" a picture. They have considerable control over their photographs and are able to illustrate their ideas precisely.

As with all aspects of craft and art, knowledge and skill enter into the use of the camera as a resource for illustration. One must consider one's knowledge, skill, and equipment before using photography for illustration. It is safe to say that anyone can make a picture and that this picture can convey graphic information more effectively than written language alone. With above-average skill one's scope is extended considerably.

To describe something or someone, nothing is easier than to show a picture. Increasing complexity requires more than average skill and ability: the need to show something that has a particular quality, such as oldness or newness, for instance, or someone doing something in a particular way. One must assess one's abilities in regard to the particular case. If greater skill is required, one should use a professional photographer. Subjects with high reflectivity, textural effect, subtle qualities, or unusual shapes or sizes are difficult even for the professional and need special equipment, knowledge, and skills in order to be captured in a picture. A simpler picture, however, can't be beat for communication value, and you can make your own easily with a camera.

Snapshots

Eastman Kodak popularized the snapshot. A great deal of information explaining how to shoot pictures, how to use the camera, and systems of photography

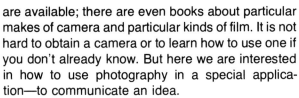

7-3. Control of lighting and exposure affects the interpretation of the subject. The subject of the two illustrations is the same; the exposure and lighting were changed to produce the different effect.

are available; there are even books about particular makes of camera and particular kinds of film. It is not hard to obtain a camera or to learn how to use one if you don't already know. But here we are interested in how to use photography in a special application—to communicate an idea.

Part of the snapshot process is the system for processing and printing the pictures. One turns in the exposed film and receives developed film and prints: the photo finishers handle this process with automated equipment and produce finely finished standard-size prints of the full negative for the lowest possible price. If your exposures are within average tolerances—and with today's cameras this condition isn't too difficult to satisfy—this system gives the best results for the most economical price. If your exposures can be improved with unusual development techniques, special printing, or cropping, you can take your film to a film-processing lab that does craftwork instead of machinework, and you will obtain better results, though at a higher price.

For craft film processing at custom labs it is usually advisable to have the film developed and printed as a proof sheet so that further work is limited to a selection of the best shots. This procedure removes photography from the snapshot classification and provides the opportunity to refine your work by selecting the best negatives and the best cropping. It also requires more skill and knowledge on the part of the photographer. But selecting the best of sev-

eral exposures is not too difficult.

"Best" is a relative term that must relate to what is required to the print in terms of its purpose. There are technical considerations, such as the density and quality of the negative, and aesthetic considerations, such as the effectiveness, interpretation, tonality, and range of the composition. Given the ability to manipulate the camera in order to produce negatives of technically acceptable quality, there are certain basic aesthetic qualities that can help you to obtain the most usable picture to illustrate an idea.

The most basic rule—and one of the most common difficulties—is to isolate the subject. Since a photo includes the background, it is important that it not confuse or distract from the subject. The photos (7-2) illustrate this concept with a picture of a leaf, first in its natural setting, in which it is difficult to identify the leaf that we are interested in, and next isolated against an appropriate and contrasting background. Whether the leaf is symbolic of people or of objects, the photo must be clear about its subject in order to communicate the idea. To take a picture of any objective subject, the picture should be composed so that the subject is isolated.

In this example it is simple enough to move the leaf to a clear space and to select a background that provides a tonal contrast. It is likewise simple to ask

7-4. Manipulation of the lens opening can also isolate the subject if the lens is powerful enough. The picture at left includes too much detail in the background; the picture at right diffuses the background through the lens focus to eliminate unwanted detail.

someone to step away from a crowd or to stand in front of a pleasingly contrasting background. If the subject is too large to move, such as a building, for instance, the photographer must move and contrive a viewing position that produces the same effect. Depending on the subject and on its location, this can call for ingenuity. Some subjects are clearly too difficult for snapshots.

These photos (7-3) show the effects of lighting and exposure for contrast. Using the same background but altering the lighting and exposure makes the leaf appear completely different in terms of color and contrast, but, if you look closely at its form and detail, you can see that it is the original leaf. More than just an image on film, the contrast of a snapshot can be controlled for its aesthetic effect.

The effect of the lighting on the form in the example is similar, but, due to a different negative density, the tonal contrast has changed.

Custom printing can interpret and control tonal range and tonal value to a certain extent, but no amount of printing control can overcome a weak or incorrectly exposed negative. Today's films offer such latitude that it is almost difficult not to get a picture, yet exact and controlled exposure, matched to lighting, is an effective tool with which to interpret the subject. The professional uses this tool with virtuosity; the amateur can also experiment with exposure. Observe the improved textural rendition in the second set of photos (7-3) as compared to the first (7-2). They should suggest that a subject that requires precise control should be turned over to the professional, who has the lighting, equipment, cameras, and setup to manipulate the exposure and print for the desired effect.

Many of today's cameras have powerful lenses, and in most cases they permit a selection of focus

7-5. The position and kind of lighting bring out different qualities in the subject. Frontal lighting, such as that from a flash bulb, brings out surface color in the photo at left, while overhead lighting, such as noonday sun, elicits form and texture in the photo at right.

and exposure. If the amateur uses a camera with a sufficiently powerful lens, he has yet another tool with which to isolate his subject. These photos (7-4) indicate that the lens can be focused so that the depth of field excludes unwanted detail by blurring the image and focuses on the subject sharply. This is accomplished by manipulating the aperture or lens opening and the speed of the camera in relation to the speed of the film: the larger the lens opening, the smaller the depth of field. The amount of light admitted by the larger opening must be compensated for by speeding up the exposure relative to the speed of the film. Film can be developed for different rates of speed—it is usually forced to faster speeds—and the professional can change film speed and processing techniques, whereas the amateur must rely on mechanized processing, which is predicated on the average.

These photos (7-5) show the effect of lighting on form. Light and shadow express form. The wood-carving of the Dutch girl (see 1-2, 1-3, 1-4, 1-5) is shown here on the doorstop. Notice that the flat lighting in the first photo interprets the shape and surface tone of the carving, while the angled lighting in the second interprets its form and texture.

The photographer works with light, the light reflected from the subject through the lens onto the film. Control of lighting is another tool to use in making a picture. Through experience one learns to observe the subject lighting in terms of the image made on film. The amateur can learn to select high or low lighting for the effect that he wants: one can shoot with the sun high or low or use the diffused light of shadowed areas, depending on the aesthetic effect wanted. The range of lighting that is acceptable to film is much smaller than that available to the eye. One must learn to interpret the detail that the

camera can "see." Again, the professional has a great advantage over the amateur in that he can use different kinds of light, control its intensity, and understand the effect that will be produced.

These photos (7-6) show how a subject can be interpreted by changing the lighting, exposure, and contrast. Though the objective subject is the same in each case, each picture brings out different emphasis. This emphasis in turn has the effect of producing a different picture subject. It is as if one picture is interested in the color, another in the form, and another in the flower. While every viewer will interpret the effect in his own way, the three pictures should make it evident, if this is necessary, that photography is capable of great variety and subtlety of interpretation, even if the camera, subject, and lighting angle are not changed.

From the foregoing discussion one point should be clear: the distinction between the amateur and the professional photographer. The amateur can obtain very satisfactory pictures and can learn to control composition, contrast, exposure, focus, and lighting to get excellent results, but the professional has techniques at his disposal that the amateur does not. This is not meant to deprecate the amateur but rather to indicate the need for discrimination. Almost anyone can expect to get serviceable pictures to express his or her ideas and with practice to make excellent pictures and to enjoy the advantage of picture making, but, if finer work is required, the services of a professional photographer should by all means be used. We have already specified that a professional is required to shoot subjects with high reflectivity, textural effect, subtle qualities, or unusual shapes or sizes: he is also required when quality is indicated. There is a clear distinction between the work of the amateur and the work of the professional.

Cropping and sizing

Glossy prints are usually preferable to mat prints for reproduction purposes, because their higher reflectivity emits more light to the reproduction camera. If work is to be printed or duplicated, one should con-

7-6. By combining various aspects of camera manipulation it is possible to increase the interpretive ability of photography. These pictures demonstrate the effect of different lighting, exposure, and background contrast on interpretation. The lighting angle, picture angle, and cropping are identical. Consider how the rose might be altered if these factors are also manipulated.

sider the end product, not the intermediary photograph used to produce the reproduction.

The normal size of a photo intended for use as art copy is 8 x 10 inches. This is not an absolute rule, but it is customary: this size allows some reduction, which enhances the reproduction, yet it is not so large as to require special protective handling or mounting. This size also relates conveniently to the 8½-x-11-inch size used for manuscript and copy sheets. For reasons of economy 5-x-7-inch photos can also be used, but it should be noted that, unless a very large quantity is involved, the savings are minimal, because the price differential between a 5-x-7-inch print and an 8-x-10-inch print is small.

Once you have the photograph that you need, it must be prepared for reproduction. It has to be cropped for the exact composition and sized for the reproduction cameraman. These two operations are necessary in order to indicate how the photo is to be used.

Cropping selects the portion of the photograph that is to be used in the design. One may use the entire picture or the portion that suits the design in which the art is to be used. The fact that the photo is a part of an overall design can influence how it should be handled.

With practice one can learn to visualize the portion that is to be used, but it is always a good idea to use right angles (7-7) to assist the visualization. They are easy to make from heavy paper or light cardboard. By moving them over the photo one can isolate the desired picture. The subject of interest can be made dominant and composed in relation to the background and to the other elements in the design.

A picture is composed by cropping. One must consider the balance and visual direction of the subject and determine how tightly or loosely to crop. Bad picture composition can be changed by cropping: only the portion indicated will be seen in the final design. In the example (7-7) the bird is too small in relation to the background. In another instance the background might be useful, but for our purpose the picture would be improved by a reduced background. The picture is composed with right angles to elimi-

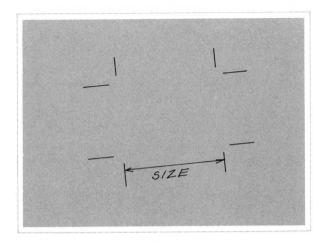

7-7. At the top left right angles are used for cropping the print. The dotted lines of the right angle and the diagonal match the proportion of the layout, and the cropping proportion is the same as the layout.

7-8. The Brandt Scaleograph at left is used for the same purpose as are the right angles (7-7). The steel bar serves as the proportional diagonal, and the plastic right angles slide to alter their position on the diagonal.

7-9. With the cropping and proportion established (above top), the picture is marked up for reproduction. This markup shows the portion of the picture to be used and the desired size.

7-10. The result of the cropping (above): only the marked portion is reproduced at the indicated size.

nate some of the background and yet to include the glow of the sun through the branches behind the bird. The proportion of the height to the depth of the rectangle is established by the crop marks.

If the photograph must fit a particular space in a design, the proportions must be maintained in the cropping relative to the space into which the photo is expected to fit. This is done with a proportion wheel on which the dimensions can be read as a percentage of reduction or enlargement. The artist who crops and sizes the picture usually uses a proportional diagonal line: the opposite corners of the space are placed directly on the diagonal line, and, no matter how large or small the opening, the proportion of height to width remains the same. The dotted lines in the example (7-7) indicate this relationship. A convenient tool for cropping pictures, which works on the principle of the diagonal line, is the Brandt Scaleograph (7-8). Two plastic right angles permit the desired portion of the photo to be framed, and the steel diagonal bar maintains the diagonal to hold the proportion.

After the desired cropping has been achieved, lines are drawn outside the picture area to indicate the cropping: they are called crop marks. They are drawn as indicated (7-9) with a soft marking pencil, such as a grease pencil, which will not damage the picture surface and which can be removed easily. These crop marks produce what is called by the printer a square halftone—square because the corners are at 90-degree right angles and halftone because the art is continuous-tone, which requires halftone-process printing.

Sizing the art consists of measuring the final reproduction size in inches and indicating it on the photograph. The size is written at the bottom or side, usually at the bottom, outside the image area and between the crop marks. The drawing (7-9) shows where the size would be indicated. The reproduction cameraman now has the information that he needs: he knows where to crop the picture and how big to shoot it. If more than one picture is used, the pictures and the corresponding locations in which they are to be used are keyed (A, B, C, etc.) with the same key letter. The photo (7-10) shows the result of the cropping-and-sizing operation.

7-11. A mask can be used to make an outline halftone. The illustration at the top shows the print and the outline-halftone mask folded back from its position over the print. The mask is used to make a separate negative that eliminates the background from the reproduction. The result is shown below. Compare this outline halftone with the square halftone (7-10).

A less common but sometimes very convenient way of using a photo is to eliminate the background entirely. This is called an outline halftone, as the subject of interest is isolated and outlined. The cropping and sizing are handled in exactly the same way as for the square halftone, but the background is eliminated by outlining the subject of interest with white paint or by making what is known as a knockout mask. The knockout mask is the preferred method, because it saves the picture and allows the reproduction cameraman some latitude in exposure. An artist can make the knockout mask in a number of ways, most conveniently with a photo-stripping material such as Ulano Amberlith. If no artist is available, the printer can do this if you instruct him as to what should be outlined. The photos (7-11) show a knockout mask attached to the photo of the bird and folded away from it. The mask outlines the bird and the branch. The cropping and sizing are the same as shown in the previous photo (7-10). The result is shown in the second photo (7-11).

Because outlining requires handwork, the outline halftone is more expensive than the square halftone. It can be the only way, however, to make use of some photographs. In other cases an outline halftone can be used more effectively than a square halftone in a design. It is a design tool.

With the use of square and outline halftones many problems of photographic composition can be handled. But it is always best to start with a good photo. No amount of cropping, sizing, or outlining can deal with some deficiencies, and the image of the subject should have the right interpretation and density of tone. Composing and cropping the photo create a new emphasis and composition; outlining the subject changes contrast; but retouching alone can change the subject.

If a change in the original size of the photo is necessary, reduction is preferred, as it improves reproduction quality. Enlargement of the original also enlarges blemishes and imperfections. Not that it is never done, but a photo that is reproduced larger than the original must be very sharp and of very high quality. It is usually better to blow up another print of the original negative. This allows a better quality of reproduction than does enlarging the reproduction.

Stock photos

Stock photos are another resource for pictures. For some reason most people are familiar with a newspaper morgue, where photos are filed for information and possible future use: stock photos serve the same purpose for public use. Stock-photo services are listed in the Yellow Pages under Photographs—Stock Shots. These businesses or agencies have extensive libraries of photographs. Many specialize in particular subject areas, and they can locate photos quickly through their system of indexing.

The advantage of stock photos is their price. It costs less to buy a stock photo than to have one shot for a special purpose. Many of the problems that one encounters with stock photos are the same as those with clip art in that the photos are generic and not specific to the subject with which you are dealing. This is mitigated to some extent by the size of the library and by the efficiency of the filing system.

In using stock photos one should specify the area as nearly as possible and select from what is available the subject that most nearly reflects the quality, feeling, or treatment needed. For example, if one wants a picture of a woman using a vacuum cleaner, it might be located in a file of models who pose with hard-line merchandize. There may be any number of pictures of a woman using a vacuum cleaner, and the selection would be made according to the special needs of the design—the character of the model, the type of vacuum cleaner, the setting and background, or the composition of the picture. Depending on the size of the library, one might have to be very specific as to the situation wanted in order to eliminate inappropriate photos. For a large file the description of a woman using a vacuum cleaner would be too general and would have to be amended with more character detail: is the woman young or mature, light or dark, in a skirt or slacks; is the vacuum cleaner a stand-up or compact model? The desired characteristics should be defined as well as the purpose.

When using stock photos, it is also advisable to be specific as to the use of the photograph and to define the use and the charges on the purchase order or contract. This can save difficulties later with

7-12. Cropping can recompose the picture and change the emphasis. This subject is altered to emphasize the church by the recropping shown below.

model releases and with additional charges for an unauthorized use. Stock photos are rented, so to speak, not purchased outright: that is, the title does not change hands. The models are paid fees for modeling and sometimes for any other use of a picture: the agency must pay this fee, and it retains the title to the picture. Some stock-photo agencies retain attorneys just to police the use of their material; to avoid future misunderstanding, be specific and abide by the contract.

The question of ownership can seem confusing, especially if the photo does not need to be returned, but it becomes clearer if you consider that the negative from which the photograph was printed is the prime property. The photographer retains the negative and any future use to be derived from it. He can make any number of prints; and, since he retains the negative, he can sell the photographic print again and again. This is why the use of a photograph does not constitute ownership of the picture. If exclusive use of the picture is desired, this must be negotiated in addition to use alone.

Most professional photographers have a file of photographs and negatives. If your need for a picture does not warrant dealing with a stock-photo agency, any number of photographers may be able to supply you with photographs from existing negatives in their possession. The photographer must retain rights to use the negative if it has already been contracted for by someone else, but most have many such pictures. The business conditions in this instance are the same as with stock-photo agencies. Make sure that you are not liable for release if models are used in the photo.

In using photography with figures one should always observe the proprieties and determine that the use of the picture does not infringe the rights of the models nor do them any injury. The people that we are so accustomed to seeing in photographs are professional models, and they are paid for their work. They are accustomed to seeing their likeness displayed in public, and they give their consent, their release, for the use of the picture in this manner. Private individuals do not, and in some instances public display can actually be harmful to them in their private lives and in their business activities: every individual has the right to privacy.

7-13. Retouching is sometimes the only answer to a photographic problem. Offending images are removed from the print by a retouch artist. The gate and the sign in the print at left are distracting: they are eliminated from the print at right.

Some subjects are ideal for stock photographs —landscapes, buildings, famous places, or famous figures, for instance. Such photos are usually available in abundance, and they are in stock-photo files because they have some particular artistic merit. If you need this kind of illustration, stock photos provide excellent quality at a much lower price than does shooting the subject specifically for your own use.

These photos (7-12) illustrate a stock photo of a church with its steeple towering into a backdrop of mountains and clouds. Cropping and composing can be used to change the emphasis of the picture. Because stock shots are professional pictures and are usually the best of a series, there is little need for retouching, although you may want to remove some

distracting element. Recourse to retouching can be expensive, but it is sometimes the only way to get what you want. These photos (7-13) illustrate such an example. If the gate in the foreground and the power line on the right are distracting for our purposes, they can be removed by retouching.

Some photographic subjects must be handled by retouching, as no amount of invention can eliminate some distracting elements. Other situations can be handled more simply by ghosting the background and letting only the subject stand out sharply. While airbrushing and retouching are jobs for an artist, one can also use a sheet of transparent material made for this purpose, available from an art-supply store. The sheet is applied to the photo and removed from the subject area; if you have the finesse for the delicate job of cutting around the subject, you can use this method. Otherwise you should let the reproduction cameraman outline the subject and use an outline halftone.

The use of stock photos brings one into contact with the professional photographer or at least with professional photographic work. It is a small jump from this level to the use of a professional photographer's services. It has been pointed out that a professional photographer should be employed for more difficult subjects and for high quality; any professional should be able to handle such an assignment, but, as in any form of artwork, there is a great range of ability and specialization to choose from. Select a photographer who specializes in the work that you want done. If you can, be specific as to the assignment; the photographer should also be able to give you an estimate.

Professional photography is available at a great variety of prices. Preeminent professionals command the highest price; most studios have a price range within which they must operate, because their setup determines their hourly costs. Less lavish setups offer lower costs. The rules for doing business are the same as for the purchase of any service. Professional photography is a service, because the product is custom-made to your specific needs.

If you know nothing about the photographer or photographic studio that you are dealing with, it can be helpful to look at samples of their work. From these examples and a brief discussion you can determine whether the photographer can provide the service that you want and the cost of such work. You can also determine whether less work and lower costs would be suitable, and referrals can be obtained simply by asking. It really isn't difficult. It should be observed that simpler work can be done surprisingly inexpensively, and you get your own art.

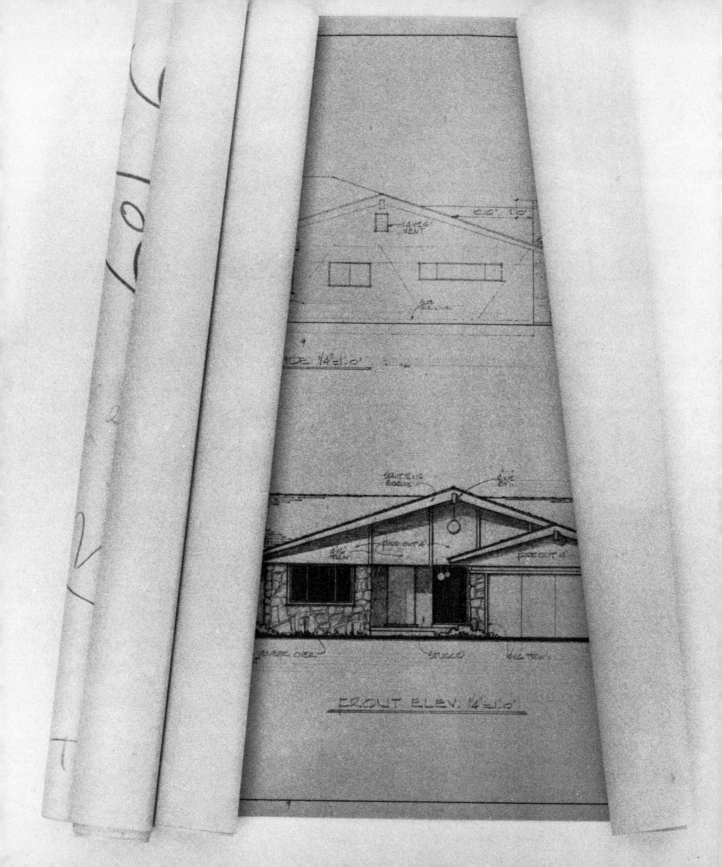

8. YOUR OWN ART

Your own art, whether design or illustration, is produced to your specifications. It particularizes your ideas. Nothing that is adapted from some other source can communicate so well, it seems, because original art has an almost indefinable quality that focuses on the essential content of the communication. If a picture can communicate more easily than words, a particular and specific picture can illustrate an idea even better.

With the many ways and means to adapt and use pictures it is not difficult to visualize the concept that is to be communicated with illustration. Specific art, done to illustrate the particular concept, is more likely to depict the idea behind the concept through the fitness of the choice and the use of symbol and metaphor. In this sense producing your own art is easier than adapting an illustration, because it takes less skill to work directly from idea to concept than to adapt the concept as well. Yet neither method is so difficult as to hinder anyone who can express himself or herself in the symbols of language.

8-1. Your own art may have many surprising applications. The elevation drawing at the bottom of this set of blueprints is one example. It might be used to make an illustration.

Photography and art illustration compose objects and ideas into graphic symbols. Photography can be very literally interpreted, but with greater skills and knowledge the objects in a photograph can be used interpretively. An expert photographer can seemingly interpret them freely to achieve the planned result and to effect the desired communication. But however freely photography can be done, it would appear that the illustrator who works with paint and brush has a still freer hand to interpret, adapt, and invent means for communication, for many symbols that we commonly use exist only in our imagination. These include things to be built, historical perspectives, and conceptual views of the scientific and technical world, which for all practical purposes cannot be photographed; at least they cannot be photographed without extensive invention and preparation. Almost anything can be done with photography, but the point is that the painter has a freer hand than the photographer and, translated into a commercial application, a less expensive one.

Both rendered and photographed illustrations have their best-suited uses. The application of each is determined by the concept used to express the idea. The ways-and-means are derived from the need for communication. If one were to try to advance a for-

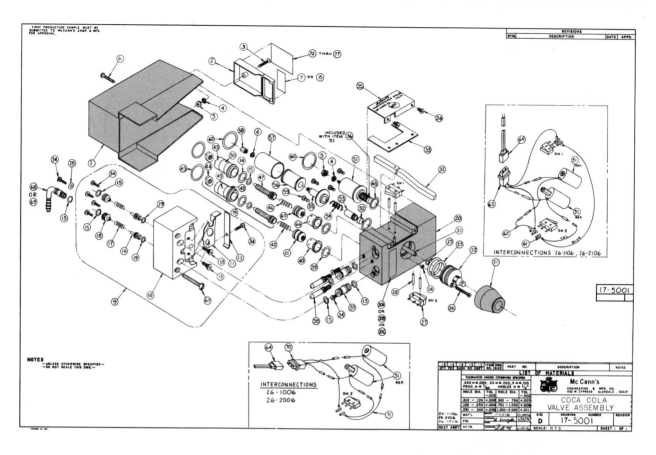

8-2, 8-3. The shaded parts of the drawing above are used to make the illustration at right. Because this is an isometric drawing—a drawing with the axis lines 120 degrees apart and no perspective—the position can be changed as desired. This is a very extreme example: most shop drawings are simpler and require less elimination of detail.

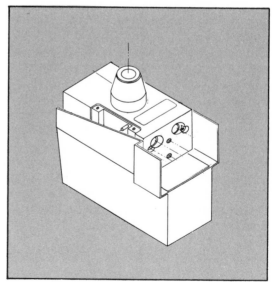

mula for this, it would be to take the simplest and most direct line to the purpose of the communication. It would involve what was most readily available, what was most economical, what was most effective.

Seen through the eyes of an illustrator, there is often a considerable amount of material available in the environment of the subject to be communicated. The drawing (8-1), a set of blueprints for a house, is an example of what can be found in a design or manufacturing environment. The portion of the blueprint that shows between the rolls is part of a rendered elevation, or, to put it more simply, a picture of one side of the house.

Such a picture could be photographed or reproduced directly when photographed as art by a reproduction camera. A picture derived from a blueprint will look like a blueprint, but for some applications it can be used appropriately. In this example, however, using the blueprint for a picture of the house has one unique advantage that should not be overlooked: it is particular and specific and conveys the uniqueness of the concept. It is not any house—it is a particular house, and the art is available. The point of the example is to emphasize the existence of such particular, specific art in the environment of the subject.

If such a subject were to be developed, the usual procedure is to obtain an architectural rendering from the blueprints. If a model has been made, as is sometimes the case, another way to further develop the illustration of the house is to photograph the model. The choice of whether to render or to photograph the model would be determined by the availability of a model, for it would be more expensive to build a model and to photograph it than to make a rendering. A decision to make a model might also be influenced by the needs of the communication. If, for the sake of discussion, there were to be a presentation to a large group of people, it might be more effective to have slides and a model on display than to use only a presentation rendering. Along with availability, cost and effectiveness enter into the considerations as to what is the best type of illustration to use.

This area of concept development is useful, even necessary to the illustrator or photographer. These are design decisions that relate to the objective; and, while the illustrator or photographer can interpret and work with your concepts and even suggest which is preferred, he can hardly be expected to make decisions for the executive. The executive must determine the objective. Concepts of objective are sometimes confused with concepts of communication, since the latter is used to convey the former.

To make your own art, there must be a base from which to work, which we are calling the objective. Without this base the artist would have to infer his own objective: if an assignment is given in this way and a concept inferred by the illustrator is clearly communicated by a picture, the executive cannot say, "But this isn't what I meant"—there was no concept of the objective to begin with. This is the reason for the sketch-and-development technique: it anchors the concept of the objective. The obvious conclusion is that for your own specific art you have to be specific, even if you are communicating abstract concepts.

The executive will not find it difficult to communicate with the developed sensitivities of the illustrator or photographer. In the initial stages of developing one's own idea it is useful to avail oneself of pictures in the immediate environment. They help not only in formulating one's own concept but also, if not suitable for the purposes of illustration, in communicating with the artist if it is determined that illustration or photography is needed in addition to what is at hand.

Unrealized potential

The material available in the environment of a subject has a potential for use as illustration. That this is often not realized is due to one's tendency to look at this material in a different way. It was produced for another purpose and we tend to associate it only with this purpose, but, by observing it from a different point of view we can use it to communicate our ideas.

The example given of using part of a blueprint to illustrate a house is typical of many products and ideas. Working drawings and design sketches are often produced in the course of developing an idea or product. While these drawings and sketches may be unfinished and are not illustrations in themselves, they can very often be adapted to the purpose of illustration, because they are usually done to explain an idea, however informally. If your needs are not so formal as to require a specially prepared illustration, the drawings and sketches themselves can be used. The adaptation consists mostly of deleting extraneous and unnecessary information.

These illustrations show how this can be done with an isometric drawing. The first (8-2) is a reproduction of the complete engineering drawing, which is reduced in size. The second (8-3) is made up of the external pieces of the item, shown at a slightly larger size. The pieces are cut from a photoprint and repositioned into their normal assembled relationship or as desired for the illustration. Because an isometric drawing has no perspective—no horizon or vanishing points—the made-up drawing can be turned to any position. This particular engineering drawing provides a view of the underside of an electric faucet for dispensing a soft drink. This same procedure can be followed with any working drawing of any item to provide a picture: the example is an extreme case, which requires considerable elimination of unwanted detail. Many working drawings are much simpler and require only that the dimensions be eliminated.

There are many varieties of engineering and working drawings. Some are very elegant, some very complex, some very pictorial; any of these or parts of these can be used for illustration by making a photocopy. When making the photocopy, the size is changed from the original to that wanted for the illustration, and the photocopy is revised. The original drawing is untouched.

Many items are developed with a considerable number of design and conceptual sketches. They are often interesting and can serve as illustration to explain an idea. These drawings (8-4) are an example of a design sketch for a building: the first is a reduced photocopy of the complete original, and the second is a cropped version to be used for illustration.

Sketches, while more interesting than working drawings, can be more difficult to handle, because they may be continuous-tone, while working drawings are almost inevitably line art. This means that material can be deleted from a sketch only by cropping, and not by moving or repositioning portions of the drawing.

This drawing (8-5) is an example of a designer's sketch for a "banana slipper"; scribblings and notes were whited out on the photocopy. This was possible because the background was pure white, which can be eliminated from the reproduction. If this were not possible, the subject could be made into an outline halftone.

If one's environment is retail rather than industrial, sketches and working drawings can be more difficult to come by, but catalogs, packaging, display, and promotional material pertaining to your subject are more available. The assumption, of course, is that the use of such material would not infringe the copyright, and using it for the purpose of promoting, explaining or developing the product would not. The photo (8-6) indicates the kind of material that is packaged with products.

With photography displays and signs can be used for illustrative material. Specific elements of a display or sign can be realigned to suit a new illustra-tive purpose, and extraneous elements can be eliminated if necessary. This illustration (8-7) shows a portion of a display on fire control, which includes a poster of a cross section of vegetation and soil composition. The second photo shows how this poster can be used for illustration. The photograph was reshot on high-contrast film by a reproduction camera, which makes it appear as line art when reduced. This is possible here because the tonal contrast between the art and the background is sufficient to permit high-contrast film to resolve the subject into line art.

Numerous examples can be offered to demonstrate the use of environmental material for illustration purposes. To make use of this material involves shifting one's viewpoint in order to reveal such materials as sources for illustration. The means by which this is accomplished technically should be clear from the examples, which involve either photocopying or photography. While these

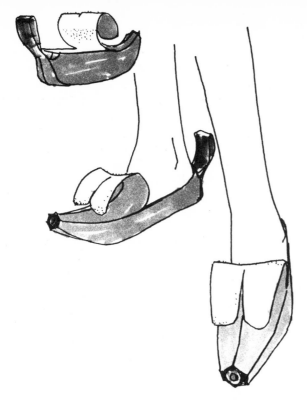

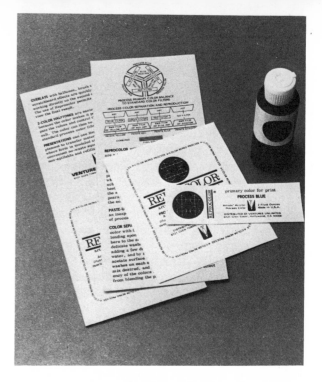

8-5. Other types of design sketches can make suitable illustrations, such as this ink and color drawing, especially if the size is reduced from the original.

8-6. In the retail environment art, packaging, and promotional material are more readily available than preliminary sketches. Most products are packaged with explanatory material.

8-7. Signs and objects in the environment can be used for illustration. With a suitable subject and a legitimate use displays such as this one might provide illustrative material. The poster at left is taken out of its display context. The line drawing, as a separate illustration, displays typical vegetation and soil drainage.

methods are not technically complex or difficult, obtaining the viewpoint is: one must develop an awareness of illustration possibilities. Becoming aware of the possibility opens the door; looking for usable material in one's environment shifts one's viewpoint; and practice develops one's ability to see a picture in terms of illustration.

Simple adaptation and utilization of legitimate and available resources through photocopying and photography can be done by anyone. The resources are there, and for many applications they provide suitable illustration. One certainly cannot argue with pertinent illustrations that enhance and clarify written ideas. Duplication and copying can be used to convey information for many purposes. If there is a need for a more developed or refined illustration, as for a broader exposure or for public promotion of a product or service, the services of a professional photographer or artist should be utilized.

Buying art

To obtain a professional illustration, one uses the services of a professional. There are many job descriptions for all the services that the professional artist or photographer provides. The most general and inclusive art field is commercial art; for professional photography the general category is commercial photography. The Yellow Pages list artists and photographers under these general titles.

With the complexities of commercial art and commercial photography professionals are increasingly becoming specialists. The commercial artist is often designated as either a designer or an illustrator. Commercial photographers also specialize in advertising and in a number of other fields. The reason, of course, is that a background knowledge of the subject is necessary in order to do professional work, because the skill of the commercial artist or commercial photographer is applied to a subject. This should not be construed to mean that the professional does not or cannot work with unfamiliar subject material but rather that he or she tends to use background knowledge as a focus for a specialty.

This enables the buyer of art to select the services of a professional who is familiar with the product, market, or subject. Depending on one's needs, this can make communication easier; it can also be a hindrance if one is looking for a novel or totally new concept. One would normally, however, work with the experienced, specialized, professional commercial artist or commercial photographer—the illustrator or advertising photographer. This can be helpful if the buyer lacks experience in buying art: to some extent the professional illustrator or advertising photographer can supply a knowledge of current methods and styles.

8-8. This photograph suggests the extent of a sign's illustrative possibilities. Because it is outlined, portions of the sign can be eliminated in the production if desired, or the photo of a street sign could be retouched with a different message.

While the commercial photographer is solely a producer of pictures, it should be noted that the commercial artist is also engaged in other activities. Design and illustration are quite different: although the buyer might need the services of a designer to produce printed and other promotional material, he would use an illustrator to produce a picture. As these services are becoming increasingly specialized, one would not necessarily be able to hire one artist to do both.

The buyer can contact an artist directly or by referral. Judgments can be made by looking at samples of work done for other clients, perhaps those similar in nature to the buyer's requirements. This photo (8-9) depicts a typical portfolio with examples of original illustration. It is up to the buyer to determine whether the approach is suitable for his needs. This is probably his most difficult decision, and it is made easier if he or she realizes that any number of professionals can provide what is needed. Differences of style are not nearly so important as is a professional execution of the communication concept, however it is interpreted. It is reassuring to realize that any number of interpretations can express and communicate the same fundamental idea, even if in different ways. The level of professionalism determines how well subtleties and nuances are controlled and related to the communication.

In some cases it can be useful to talk to the illustrator or photographer directly, but in many instances the buyer's requirements are communicated through a third party, such as an agent, a studio sales representative, or a designer. In each case the third party is an expert who assists both the buyer and the illustrator or photographer. All parties involved are vitally interested in obtaining a successful result.

It is customary to give a purchase order or memo describing the work to be done, which can include the price and specify other conditions; it is also customary, when a working relationship has been established, to gloss over formalities. This seems to grow out of the working relationship and is influenced by the personalities involved and by the policies of a particular business. The more people involved in a project, the more complicated and expensive the work becomes. If a working relationship has been established over a period of time, it is

actually possible for an experienced art buyer, art director, or designer to give an assignment over the phone. This, of course, is based on mutual respect, knowledge, and very good communication among parties.

The time involved in doing the work is a substantial factor in the charges. Other factors are the scale of charge, or the rate, and the overhead. Professional work is not automatically or necessarily expensive: it can become expensive, but the charges depend on what is required, how the buyer goes about buying the art, and the level of professionalism that he selects. Buying art is no different from buying any other service.

It is most important that the buyer form a concept of his needs. This concept establishes the scale of charges. It should be clear, for example, that the costs will be higher for a full-color illustration than for a black-and-white drawing, because the former is more difficult and time-consuming and because it requires a greater degree of skill. The same is also true in regard to the complexity of subject that is required. These factors, which the buyer's concept controls, are fundamental to cost: while a professional illustration can be inexpensive, it can also be made very expensive by a demand for time-consuming and difficult work. If a budget must be met, it is advisable for the buyer to be somewhat flexible in regard to the means used to illustrate his concept. The professional can undoubtedly recommend means of achieving the objective within the framework of the budget. Inflexible needs will inevitably result in set illustration costs, which the budget must meet, but in other instances adjustments can be made by adapting the illustration requirements to the needs of the buyer.

The buyer's concept also affects the level of professionalism required to do the illustration. It is entirely possible to use a lower-cost service if the work is suitable. As in any field, the illustrator and the photographer tend to command prices for their work in accord with the level of their skills: the higher the skills, the higher the price. It is not cost-efficient to use a highly paid skill to do a job that does not make use of that skill. Lesser requirements can be done at a lower price.

The application of this principle to art requires experienced judgment and, of course, can be most efficiently handled by the professional art director, designer, or art buyer, who can find just the right applications for different talents. For a less skilled art buyer who must rely more heavily on the support of the professional a conservative position of aiming just a little too high is safer, but this also means paying more for the insurance. Each executive will find a balance in the expertise of his field, for, to be sure, no one knows the needs of the communication better than the executive who is buying the illustration. This is a signal for the inexperienced art buyer to use his judgment under advisement yet to be firm in his concept of the requirements for the outcome. This is the best position, for it allows the professional the greatest latitude in interpretation and alternatives but assures that the end result will be effective, something that concerns everyone involved.

In principle the purchase of illustrative art and photography is the same, but each has different capabilities and requirements, and a knowledge of these is useful to the buyer. As is often the case, the requirements of the communication and the mechanics of producing a picture help determine whether art or photography should be used. If it is a matter of interpretation, then either can be used to reach the same end. With a flexibility of concept, the cost scale for alternative methods would include black-and-white art at the low end, photography in the middle, and full-color illustration at the high end, with some mechanically elaborate photography even more expensive. This scale of value can be overbalanced by the use of highly reputed illustrators and photographers for the sake of their unique contribution. The art buyer is paying for their point of view and notoriety, yet this can be worthwhile in the right application.

The business practices involved in buying art are

8-9. Portfolios come in all sizes and shapes. Some artists and agents prefer to display their art on slides, but this typical portfolio contains the original art.

in accord with established standards. If you commission work, you are obligated to pay for what you have commissioned. Do not expect a professional to work on spec. The more extensive the use of the picture, the higher the price. Be exact as to the intended use of the illustration, because if you use it more extensively, the illustrator can claim a larger fee. A painting may now be copyrighted without publication. This is done by registering the work with the copyright office upon completion, which involves sending a fee, information, and a photograph of the work to Washington, D.C. While the photographer never sells his picture outright, the artist may do so, but he or she does not relinquish the right to residual payment for subsequent use.

In dealing with the professional the art buyer operates much as he would with any other business. There is no mystery, and aesthetic generalities can be resolved as to specific needs in commercial applications. These are the needs of communication in terms of sales, engineering, or a host of other applications. The buyer is not in the dark as to the concept involved: he is the generic formulator of the concept, and much of the success of the communication is derived from the exactness and perspicacity of this objective. This should make it easier for the expert executive but novice art buyer to deal with the vagaries of art. The executive can perceive his or her central role in the commissioning and execution of illustration and photography: the illustrator and photographer are telling the story as they understand it from the executive, and the purposes of the executive are central to the success of the project of which communication with illustration and photography is a part.

Communication

Public communication is sometimes criticized because it is designed for the twelve-year-old, sometimes because its jingo and jargon are unnecessarily complex. Communication carries the burden of attitude and not necessarily an attitude that is related to content. The means of communication would ideally be designed to serve the content of the idea. Both sender and receiver bring attitudes to it, but the communication should be as pure as possi-

ble. To achieve this goal, simplification is a virtue.

Communication designed for the twelve-year-old is misconceived. The attitude of talking down to your audience is a mistake on the part of the communicator. It is, however, well established and proven that the audience is more receptive to the simpler communication. It is not a matter of talking down but of presenting the idea as simply as possible in order to benefit the communication. The twelve-year-old level is really a median level in a theoretical yardstick of complexity. A better interpretation is that the twelve-year-old is capable of understanding and that the burden is on the communicator to present the idea well enough to avoid ponderous reasoning and the antagonistic jingo of ego-satisfying jargon.

The recipients of the communication may well be able to understand it, but why should they have to work so hard, and why would they want to? Complex communications on complex subjects filled with complex abstractions are, in a word, complex. These communications can ideally be made plain, and this would take nothing away from their content or their benefits to the recipient. The use of pictures is advocated as a means of achieving simplicity.

8-10, 8-11, 8-12. These three atmospheric illustrations deal with the subject of communication: abstractly (left), generically (center), and specifically (right). The art at left was based on a photo of a sculpture entitled *The Family* by David Green, commissioned by Lytton Savings; the art in the center is a pen-and-wash drawing; the art at right is a photograph that takes advantage of a sign situation.

The broadest concept has the widest appeal. Opening up the idea need not lack particularity nor specificity: a communication should appeal to the broadest sphere of interest. These illustrations (8-10, 8-11, 8-12) show the use of abstraction in a simple communication: in the first it is used primarily as atmosphere to add interest; the second is a generic symbol of the theme; the third is a specific symbol of the theme. There is a delicate balance of idea between the poetry of the personal and the unique and the content of universal appeal. The motive for the communication has much to do with this. One may safely assume that the recipient has a high level of intelligence but a low level of motivation to understand. The floods of media and the self-serving motivations of much communication make the reason for this clear.

Accurate information and transfer are essential to business, to bourgeoisie and buyer alike. The concepts that we develop about ourselves and our environment are often predicated on the information that we have. These concepts have to do with all kinds of things—such as places where we have never been, objects that we have never seen, and ideas that we have not proven. The invention of concepts from false information can only lead to confusion and disillusionment; the transfer of such data makes the nonexistent appear self-propelling.

Real communication is more than relaying information: the information should have meaning and purpose. Information plus perception with insight equals communication. The difference between information and communication is the difference between concept and idea: a concept can be understood, but an idea can be experienced. This implies that, for an idea to be communicated, there must be insightful perception. It puts the idea beyond the reach of the concept used for the communication. Information is not insight. Conversely, it also implies that there can be no insight if the information or concept used for the communication is not true. We almost automatically assume that concepts must represent an idea; we make ourselves the servants of concepts instead of ideas, which can allow any system of concepts to proliferate. Real communication contains ideas.

Substanceless communication lacks ideas. An example is the kind of advertising that says that the product is more but fails to say more than what or that says that it is bigger, better, newer when to limit comparison to "er" is to err. It might be just as effective to picture the product and the name. Uncompared comparisons and similar incomplete assertions are puffs without meaning of their own. They borrow meaning by association and are designed to borrow on credit, the credit that we might unthinkingly lend them. Such advertising is just shelf space in the media.

Substanceless communication is like a conversation punctuated by "you know" in which an interpretation is missing and the sympathy of the listener doesn't require it. It is an image of a shared attitude; perhaps the sympathy is the communication, and the real meaning is nonverbal.

Public information for proletarian proliferation benefits from communication as a mental image. If slogans are successful, images pictured on TV are more so, as TV demonstrates. The mental image is constructed: it is not the result of insight, and it is not necessarily true. The communication concept is to produce the image in people's minds by picturing the image. Slogans make images in people's minds, and so do pictures. The force of TV is probably due to its pictures, because pictures don't have to say too much, nor do they take too long to say it. With the construction of the mental image you can have the cake and eat it too. With the image in mind whatever is associated with it assumes its identity no matter what the facts are, because the message has already been communicated.

This is substanceless communication with pictures, but it points to the ethics of communication. Such communication doesn't really communicate, because the mental images, the picture concepts, have no foundation in idea. Whether the communication concepts are presented with words or with pictures, the perception of the concepts should lead to insight into the idea. This demonstrates the role of motive and attitude in communication: why is the communication done in this way? Whether simple or complex, appealing or ponderous, verbal or illustrative, the concept must connect to an idea for communication to exist. With perception there can be insight, which presents the idea and completes the purpose of communication. But for this to occur, the concepts must be true in their relationship to the idea. With this view of communication the ethics are built in. The communication cannot be completed if there is nothing, no idea, being communicated. It is like saying, "Is the image real, a concept used to communicate a real idea; or is the image a construction, a concept used to convey another concept—is it idea or is it imagination?"

Communication should ideally be simple, appealing, accurate, and real. With the increasing scope and complexity of our society we need good communication more than ever. Reprographics, techniques and devices to use for communication, are available as never before. All can be used with pictures as well as with words. The use of pictures can simplify, appeal, and contribute to the accuracy and substance of communication: pictures are a graphic means for graphic communication.

8-13.

Signs of our times: Hollywood is still the film capital, but much film production is now linked to the communications giant, television. Klieg lights, center stage, dress up the sign with Hollywood's "genuine illusion" of glamour, while towering above in the darkness is one of the first TV antennas.

SECTION III:

HANDLING OF ILLUSTRATION

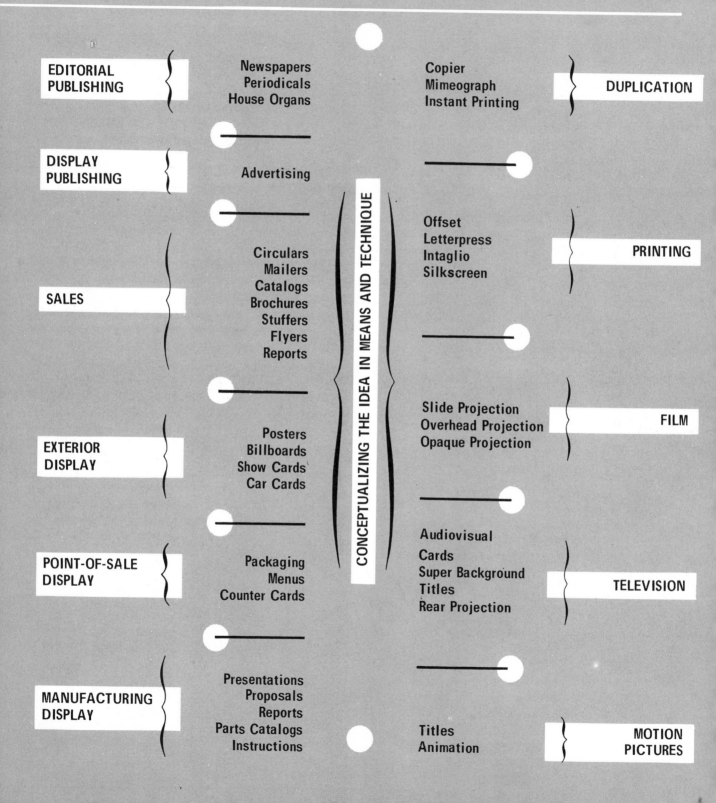

MEDIA FOR ILLUSTRATION

PROCESSES & TOOLS FOR ILLUSTRATION

EDITORIAL PUBLISHING

Newspapers
Periodicals
House Organs

Copier
Mimeograph
Instant Printing

DUPLICATION

DISPLAY PUBLISHING

Advertising

PRINTING

Offset
Letterpress
Intaglio
Silkscreen

SALES

Circulars
Mailers
Catalogs
Brochures
Stuffers
Flyers
Reports

CONCEPTUALIZING THE IDEA IN MEANS AND TECHNIQUE

EXTERIOR DISPLAY

Posters
Billboards
Show Cards
Car Cards

Slide Projection
Overhead Projection
Opaque Projection

FILM

POINT-OF-SALE DISPLAY

Packaging
Menus
Counter Cards

Audiovisual
Cards
Super Background
Titles
Rear Projection

TELEVISION

MANUFACTURING DISPLAY

Presentations
Proposals
Reports
Parts Catalogs
Instructions

Titles
Animation

MOTION PICTURES

9. DISPLAY ADVERTISING

Using pictures also means handling them in a way that meets mechanical requirements. The need to handle illustration is now a part of more executive functions than ever before. The reason is that illustration is a part of the intrabusiness graphic-communication process. The need at least for executive direction of message content is clear, and this involves the executive on a need-to-know basis.

Sales constitute the bulk of illustration usage, and the business executive must deal with pictures or with the artist and the photographer. Advertising takes many forms. Next in volume are engineering and manufacturing requirements, such as proposals and presentations, in which communications are devoted primarily to explaining and presenting an idea. Intrabusiness communications are primarily concerned with selling an idea. The publishing of books, periodicals, and catalogs primarily involves communications professionals because of the amount of work involved. Writers and editors are or must become experienced in dealing with pictures, artists, and photographers and conversant with the techniques involved.

Display advertising is picture advertising. It is an entry area into graphic communication for many executives, whether for retail sales or for intra-business communications. Communications play a major role in the executive function. Because graphic communications are only part of this function, many executives are limited in their knowledge of graphic means, which can severly limit their efforts and their use of pictures for communication.

Understanding the large array of uses for illustration in the various forms of display advertising and publishing, as shown in the diagram (9-1), is a formidable task. It is the responsibility of the specialist, the illustrator or communications expert. The executive needs to understand enough to avoid confusion among the innumerable technicalities and variations and to conceptualize. He or she primarily needs to understand the structure and availabilities of the graphics field. A broad general knowledge of the means of communication, of the state of the art, assists the executive in developing his concepts.

Each field of graphics has its specialists and experts, and the user must to a great extent rely on the expert for specific and detailed requirements. Each graphic house has its own view of the specifics. But this is not a problem, because the executive is himself an expert in grasping the fundamentals of a project and in delegating authority.

Working with communication can be seen in

terms of delegating authority: the essential message formulated by the executive is delegated to the communication experts for development. The executive must formulate the concept and retain sufficient control to assure the content of the message and must balance this responsibility by allowing the specialist sufficient freedom to make the most of his talent and skills in producing the communication. The executive chooses the specialists and understands how to use pictures for communication.

If this role seems impersonal, we must remember that in this age of service specialists even presidents no longer write their own speeches. Lincoln wrote the Gettysburg address, but modern presidents employ speechwriters, yet we feel that the speech expresses the president's meaning.

The difficult aspect of the executive's job is to select the medium or combination of media for communication and to handle pictures for that medium or combination. ("Media" is the plural of "medium" and also the popular term for public communications in general.) To deal with this very simply, as the executive must do, the fundamentals of the communication medium can be viewed as both a vehicle and a tool. The photo (9-2) shows a billboard, which is a vehicle of communication; the drawing (9-3) shows a slide projector for audiovisuals, which is a tool; but in reality both are vehicle and tool. This is like saying that a car is both a means of transportation and a machine. To give a specific example, a newspaper is both a communication medium and printing.

The media use various technologies, each of which places different requirements on the graphics and on the use of pictures. This is the choice of mechanical requirements.

The executive or user is thus responsible for three decision-making areas: the choice of the graphic means used to communicate with his audience, the choice of media, and the choice of technology. These can be called the three m's: means, media, and mechanics. It is probably better for the executive to know too little rather than too much, for it is said that a little knowledge is a dangerous thing, but the executive does need to know.

Graphic means

The means of graphic communication can be anything from a note to one person to a television message to millions. The note might be scrawled on a piece of paper and signed with a happy face, while the television graphics might involve a complicated process such as animation, which has layers of technology. The choice of means has to do with concept: how the message should be communicated, to whom, and why.

Judgments must be made as to how to simplify the communication and illustrate the idea and as to what level of polish is necessary for the graphics to be effective in the given situation. With more formalized and expensive undertakings there are also considerations of the effect of the vehicle and the method and of how they relate to the image of the communication in the mind of the recipient. This choice might be compared to deciding whether to send the message over in a pickup truck or in a limosine.

The choices have to do with the objectives, with company policy, and with the projection of a public image. These considerations can be very subjective, but they affect the content of the message as

9-2, 9-3. The photograph at right shows a communication vehicle, the medium of outdoor advertising; the drawing below, also of a communication vehicle, depicts an audiovisual unit made by IAV/Standard. Although both the billboard and the audiovisual unit are used for communication, they have a completely different character.

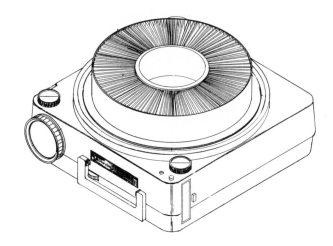

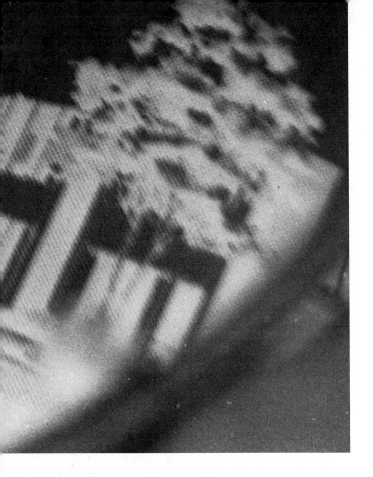

9-4. Film is used with the halftone process to make a Velox. A Velox is necessary to reproduce tonal art with duplication processes, because they reproduce the printing element directly without the use of negatives. A halftone cannot be made with duplication equipment. This magnified photo shows the dots on the halftone negative used to make a Velox print.

well as the use of illustration. One very important effect of these considerations is to determine how much money should be budgeted for the communication. Another is to determine how much labor is to be devoted to the communication. The colorations of these decisions also affect the selection of photography or art and of what kind of art, as this relates to its effect on the communication. This effect is sometimes considered more important than the mechanics of workability. These decisions are influenced to a great degree by merchandising and sales themes, by the market, and by how the market is to be approached.

Graphic media

Pictures relate to the media selected for communication in a number of ways. The need for a very large picture has to be handled differently than the need for a small picture. Art suitable for a billboard might be reduced in size for print, but the reverse is not necessarily true. The main point about enlarging is that the art be of high enough quality and sufficiently refined to stand the enlargement. In the normal frame of reference art for print is reduced in size from the original in the reproduction to minimize irregularities and imperfections. With billboards, posters, and art that is projected from film to a much larger size, this frame of reference is reversed and imperfections are enlarged: art that is to be enlarged therefore needs to be done in a refined manner.

The characteristics of the art enter into this consideration, because in some cases art needs to look mechanical, while in others a stylistic sketchiness can enhance the communication. This is especially true of photography in that a 4-x-5-inch print can look deceptively acceptable but, when enlarged to billboard size, lose sharpness and tonal separation. The strength of the light and the kind of screen used affect the quality of a projected picture. The projection equipment and the screen should be used within the limits of their design for the best effect. For overhead and opaque projection this is critical.

Billboards and posters make strict and sometimes awkward compositional demands because of the mechanical requirements of sheet size that must be adhered to in producing them. Television and film projection likewise have rigid proportions that the composition must follow. This problem can call for an ingenious solution if, for example, you want to get a good display of the Statue of Liberty in the horizontally elongated frame of a billboard. It is also notable that the vertical printed-page format is the opposite of the horizontal slide and television format.

Another way in which the selection of pictures should be considered is in terms of their reading speed. Only the published picture has an indeterminate reading speed, though people seem to leaf through periodicals quite rapidly. All other uses of pictures and graphics must be seen in relation to a viewing-time span. This also applies to manually operated slide viewing, because a long screening time is considered bad policy for keeping audience interest. A schematic drawing used in an overhead projector or opaque projector for technical presentation might be the exception, but in this case interest is often maintained by using a pointer to follow the discussion; in both slide situations the audience attention can leave the screen and go to the speaker.

The eye moves through a picture just as it does from picture to picture. If there is too much reading material—more than a few words—the viewer will simply ignore it. A viewer has to have a sufficient promise of reward or motivation to read, especially if narration overlaps the reading material.

Graphic mechanics

A conceptual view of mechanics distinguishes between film graphics and print graphics. In print graphics there is the additional distinction between line art and halftone art already emphasized, while film graphics includes all types of subject matter. What applies to film also applies to television, for television uses film.

The executive relies on the expertise of specialists for the most part, but recognizing the major mechanical distinctions is necessary in order to see and utilize his own resources. The executive should understand the general process required to translate this resource into one application or another, even if the actual work and art are done by the expert and the professional, because his choices determine the graphic follow-through. The executive is intimately involved, because it is his idea and concept that are being expressed.

Recognizing the different kinds of art required by print or film and the time and labor required for each process can simplify the work. There must be sufficient time for the labor involved to reach the objective. This helps in the planning process and reduces costs.

As has been shown, each process is translatable into another through photographic manipulation: that is, artwork can be made into slides; slides can be made into printed material. The ability to recognize line art means that the executive knows that this art can be printed directly without the use of the

halftone process: in a practical application—for instance, a schematic diagram—the executive knows that this line art can be printed but that it cannot be reduced for the printed-page size and still be readable and that it might be made into a slide or whatever is needed for the communication.

Color can be used for all media if the means requires it, but, because the mechanics are more complex, the costs are considerably higher than for black-and-white art. In the print media color can be considered both as full-color and as the addition of only one color, as can overhead projection; film, however, is usually handled only as black-and-white or as full-color. For print media the addition of a second color can be thought of as an additional printing of black-and-white art in color overlaid on a previous printing: thinking of color in this way makes the mechanics of the process easier to understand.

Beyond the preliminary planning stage the use of the professional, expert, or specialist makes further technical knowledge on the part of the executive unnecessary. In the area of reprography for intrabusiness communication, however, the executive can benefit from more technical understanding, as it allows him to prepare work directly for duplication. Because of its directness the executive may not have the assistance of the professional, expert, or specialist. The simplest explanation of the mechanics of reprography is that art should always be handled as line art. This means that, if the user has a photograph or any other kind of continuous-tone art, it should be translated into line art by getting a Velox print from a reproduction-camera service.

Duplication

The duplication process used for graphic material can be anything from a carbon copy to printing. Duplication printing is distinguished from job printing, as it is a much simpler process than custom work and provides a lesser degree of quality. The umbrella term for the numerous duplication techniques and processes is "reprography." Only for more formalized messages and stringent requirements is job printing used: the majority of intrabusiness graphic communication is handled with reprography.

Reprographic processes provide duplication with

varying degrees of quality. No reprographic equipment actually duplicates the original in full detail. For this you have to use job printing, in which there are only slight changes from the first printed piece to the last. Reprography is designed to copy the information if not the appearance of the original and to retain or to convey it to where it is needed.

All duplication processes can copy a picture; if you trace the outline with a stylus, even carbon paper can be used. But a carbon outline of the image is not quite the same as the original, even if it does convey the same information. Reproduction quality is a major factor in the duplication of art. The fact that reprography is designed to deal only with line and not with shades of gray requires that one make a halftone Velox, which is line art, if tonal art or photographs need to be duplicated. The photo (9-4) shows the film negative used to make the Velox. Although some copiers—namely, the electrostatic type—can handle tonal copy with some success, the translation of tonal copy into line copy allows the process to work at its optimum level.

The trade name Xerox has become almost synonymous with copying, which is interesting, because the electrostatic copying process at first seemed the least likely to succeed due to its technological complexity. The electrostatic copying process is now offered by other manufacturers as well as Xerox and has become popular because of qualities such as copy quality, cost, convenience, and availability. Copies are made by a number of processes, which are classified as wet and dry processes. The wet processes are: diazotype, diffusion-transfer, and stabilization. The dry processes are: thermal, dual-spectrum, and electrostatic. The dry processes are naturally more convenient than the wet, because the copy emerges ready for use, and those with less operations are faster.

Electrostatic copiers have the advantage of permitting copies to be made on any paper, although some papers work better than others. This can be useful if copies are needed on stationery or other preprinted paper. Tinted paper can also be used, as can papers with subtle textures. At greater cost a full-color copy process is also available, and copies can be made from film as well as color masters. Some electrostatic copiers can also change the size of the original.

To reproduce art with the electrostatic copier, it is mounted with other material on the master sheet. Copies show paper edges pasted down on the master sheet, so they should be trimmed evenly and squarely so that the shadow does not detract from the appearance of the art but rather frames it like a border. Since the copier responds only to black, it does not read whited-out corrections, provided that the whiting out corresponds to the background tone: any significant difference will appear on the copy.

Thermal and diazotype copiers can be used to copy art and to make transparencies for overhead projection. The transparency is made with fluid carbon on the thermal copier; it can then be used as a fluid master to make copies before it is used as a projected image. With the thermal copier a speaker can make a visual transparency and supply each of his listeners with a copy. The diazotype process can accommodate larger than stationery-size originals. It differs from other copying processes, however, in that the copy image is formed by passing light through the master and not by reflecting light from the master. This means that anything that disturbs, alters, or prevents light from passing through will show on the original.

Because copy machines can be very expensive if they incorporate all the functions of automatic feed, size change, collating, color duplication, and other features, many businesses use a simpler machine that makes only a same-size notepaper copy. More complex and extensive jobs, such as reproduction camerawork, photocopies that use a film negative, stabilization-paper copies that must be dried flat on a drying drum, or extensive diazotype copying of blueprints (the ammonia used in the developing process can have too strong an odor for an office), are sent out to specialists. These speciality suppliers often offer other services such as bindry with collating or photo-lab work with photocopying.

It is easy to expect too much from an office copier. While it is economical to use a copier for a few copies, a larger number becomes uneconomical, because the price per copy is too high and does not

9-5. This schematic diagram of the paste-up process, which can be used for duplication, shows how the material is assembled, manufactured, mounted, and arranged in the paste-up.

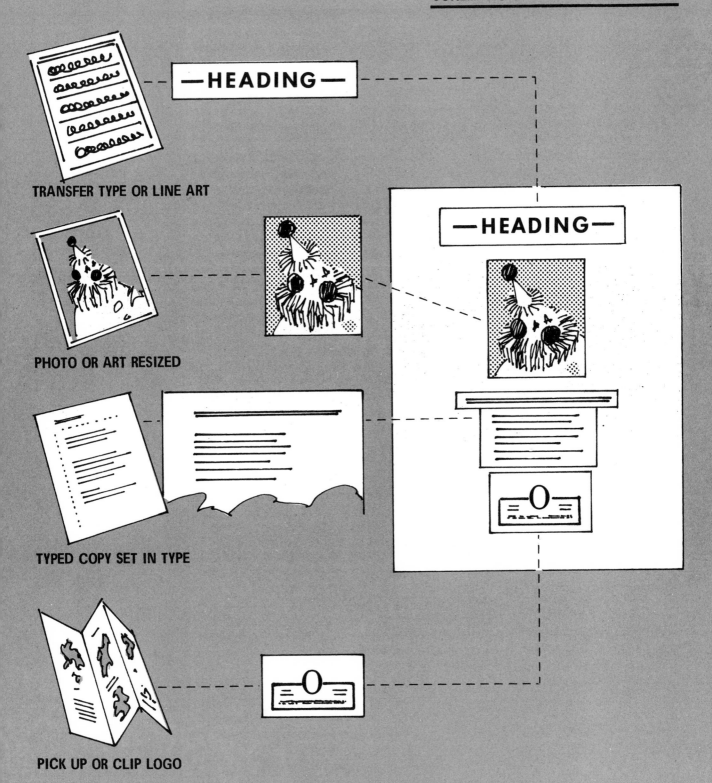

TRANSFER TYPE OR LINE ART

PHOTO OR ART RESIZED

TYPED COPY SET IN TYPE

PICK UP OR CLIP LOGO

drop with volume. The copier pays for itself by saving labor, the labor of having to do something over for the sake of a record or for different recipients.

To produce a larger number of copies, as for a mailing or a presentation for a number of people, it is more economical to use a duplicating process instead of a copier. Duplication-printing processes use some form of master or printing element to make the copies. The forms are: the fluid process, the stencil process, and the offset process. Because labor is the biggest expense and because with more copies appearance is more important, the stencil and offset processes have gained in popularity. Offset duplication is the darling of reprographics and its use is expanding rapidly, because the appearance of the reproduction copy is very much like printing—in fact, it *is* printing. With instant printing the reproduction can look better than the original! This is especially true if the original has corrections and patches or incorporates pasted art material. This fact is obviously a great advantage in terms of laborsaving, and it also means that material can be assembled with the paste-up method. Offset simplifies the handling of art and in principle utilizes the same method as that used to prepare art for the more refined job printing.

The stencil process also offers this advantage if the master, the stencil used for printing, is made with an electronic scanner. With ever-increasing labor costs it is to be expected that users of the stencil process will increasingly use a scanner to make the stencil rather than the handwork cutting method of typing on it or drawing on it with a stylus. The stencil used with the scanner also makes accurate copies of art and of any tonal copy that has been Veloxed, preferably with a halftone screen not finer than 85 lines to the inch.

The difference between the stencil duplicating process and the offset duplicating process lies essentially in the printing element used to produce the copies. The two can be compared in terms of cost and quality. To put it very simply, the stencil costs less to make but its edge is not as clean as the photographically made edge of the offset-printing element. The image duplicated by the stencil process is therefore not so sharp or clean in appearance as the image duplicated by the offset process: in short, the stencil process is cheaper; the offset process gives better quality.

The processes are comparable in that, as long as a scanner is used to make the stencil, both stencil and offset duplication can use paste-up to produce the original, and both can reproduce line art. The use of a screened halftone for tonal art, a Velox, is necessary to maintain fidelity of tone with the original art: direct reproduction of tonal art does produce some kind of image, but light tones are lost and dark tones are interpreted as black. A Velox may be thought of as a copy of the original tonal art that is incorporated into the paste-up.

The use of a paste-up permits a pleasing arrangement of the elements to be duplicated. The drawing (9-5) represents a schematic diagram of the paste-up method. It allows the incorporation of any graphic matter that has strong tonal contrast. It makes the use of art and illustration simple, and the Velox, or halftone-copying step, permits the art to be resized to meet the desired specifications. All these features allow great flexibility in composing the material: mistakes can be corrected; material can be added to or deleted from the source; the time and labor of making an original for duplication are eliminated. The assembled paste-up becomes the original. No matter what pieces from other originals are included, the duplication process copies only the dark tone.

Some systems of platemaking for offset duplication permit size changes from the paste-up to the copy. Because this is a duplication process, however, the sizes and colors are standardized. The more customized the process, the closer it approaches job printing. Color printing can be done at a cost by an instant printer. Other services may also be provided, but they share the complexity and cost of job printing.

The use of the offset process, while very desirable for business duplication, is too complex for the average office. For good results the operation of the small printing press takes more than nominal skill. If it were as easy as pressing a button, the machine would

9-6. The reproduction camera looks vastly different from our typical image of a camera. Its size permits large pieces of art to be handled and exposures to be made on large pieces of film. This camera contains a halftone screen and is used to make halftone negatives for a Velox print.

probably find its way into the office, but it isn't.

Again, as with copiers, some offset machines are fully automated, but, like automated copiers, the economic justification for such expense is lacking in most business requirements. One can buy a great deal of custom printing for the amount needed to purchase an automated machine. Unless the business is large or requires extensive duplicating, it is generally more economical to let the specialist buy the machine and maintain it and to buy from him than to maintain in-house offset duplication. This fact accounts for the sizable speciality-duplication business of instant printing.

Job printing

Job printing uses different techniques than instant printing or duplication printing. It uses film to make the printing element, and film permits a extensive manipulation and maintains greater fidelity. There is a selection of paper and of machinery to perform all kinds of custom fabrication, and the machinery is designed to maintain very fine control of the printing process.

Job printing is used when one's requirements go beyond the range of reprography in terms of quantity, custom fabrication, or quality of reproduction. Reprography systems are designed to produce from a few copies to several hundred; job-printing systems are designed to handle from a thousand to many thousands of pieces. Reprography deals with one copy at a time, but job printing prints multiples of the copy to produce the specified quantity at a higher rate of speed. Reprography handles every copy according to the design of its system; job printing is designed to handle work individually. This allows for different paper, different copy sizes, multiple colors, or full-color printing. Job printing can fold, collate, trim, bind, and finish the work. Reprographic systems simplify quality considerations to a general optimum; job printing is designed to optimize each step according to the requirements of each job.

Instant-printing reprography is designed to fill the production space between a few copies and the larger quantities of job printing. It is capable, however, of runs into the thousands and of providing a large variety of custom work: color work can be done, and many job-printing operations can be at-

tached to the system. This can be a great convenience to the user, although he should be aware of the limits of the system and of the intention of its design.

The custom fabrication of job printing is cheaper for large quantities, and the quality is better than that of reprographics. The user should realize that this is the result of the system design and that job printing is designed to be cost-efficient with quantity. With large quantities the cost per unit can be brought below anything that reprography can provide; at the same time the quality is improved by custom preparation of the job. To the buyer this means that, if the quantity is greater than several hundred copies, if a number of steps are required for fabrication, and if the best quality is necessary, he or she should compare reprography and job-printing prices or move to job printing for the sake of better quality.

Job printing can meet every conceivable need; all kinds of systems and machine designs are available. The systems are categorized into four methods of printing: offset printing, letterpress printing, intaglio printing, and silkscreen printing. With each the user is dealing with experts; their advice and counsel are available for the asking. It is appropriate to ask for estimates, especially if the user is not sure of which method to use. Specialists can usually provide the best work at the lowest prices.

Offset printing, or lithography, as it is generically termed, is the most popular method of job printing, and it is the most universally flexible and the least expensive for a number of reasons. Chief among these reasons is the fact that the offset-printing plate is mechanically simpler and costs less to prepare than the printing element used for the other methods. Recent developments in photography and improvements in the offset-printing plate permit it to produce large quantities, over two hundred thousand, and thus extend the range of offset printing. Offset printing is rapidly becoming the most used printing method.

Art is prepared for offset printing by the paste-up method. The user can prepare art for offset job printing just as he or she would for reprography. There are, however, more possibilities, and paste-ups can be done in a number of ways. If the work is at all complicated, it is usually advisable to have the help of a commercial artist. This provides better quality and results in lower overall printing costs, since the artist, in this instance a paste-up artist, can do preparatory work that the printer would otherwise have to do in a more difficult and expensive way. For offset printing paste-up is a simpler and less expensive way of assembling the art than film stripping: the user should bear this in mind and look at paste-up costs in relation to overall printing costs and not as an art cost in addition to the printing cost.

The originator can design and paste up his own work for job printing just as he might do for instant printing, but, as quality is often a prime consideration, he may want to utilize the services of a designer to produce a design for the piece in addition to a paste-up. The design factor is often confusing in terms of the cost of a printed piece. Design is a separate element; it can be applied to and incorporated into anything from a piece put through a copier for one copy to a piece with a print run in the thousands. The design question should be examined in terms of whether the additional cost is necessary to meet the expectations of the originator. Paste-up, on the other hand, is not design: it is the preparation of a design for printing, which, if not done, must be handled by the printer with film stripping in the offset process. The confusion ensues from the fact that a design can be presented as a paste-up.

The printer supplies the printing; the originator must supply what is to be printed. This is how paste-up enters into the design. The user may assemble the pictures and typesetting—the paste-up—himself, or he may provide them for the printer to assemble. Offset printers do not supply typesetting—no printers do. The job of typesetting and of arranging the type for printing is a separate function even in the older method of letterpress printing, in which these operations seem to be one because the assembled metal elements are used for printing—offset printing uses only the image. The design does not exist until the work is assembled into a design: letterpress represents the design as assembled pieces of metal; offset represents the design as a paste-up. The design must be supplied by the originator, the printer, the typesetter, or the designer.

For offset printing the paste-up is shot with the reproduction camera to make the printing plate. This photo (9-6) shows the large reproduction camera in its darkened setting next to the film-processing darkroom. Every job-printing method uses the reproduction camera to make the printing element. Offset printing uses it to make the printing plate; letterpress printing uses it to make engravings for printing; intaglio printing uses it to make the printing rollers; silkscreen printing uses it to make the printing screen.

Although offset printing is growing in popularity, letterpress printing can be more convenient for some job-printing requirements. One convenience is that the letterpress printer prints from type: this means that the typesetting can be obtained at the same location as the printing. If the printing involves only typesetting, not pictures, this is convenient; but, if pictures are used, the letterpress printer, unlike the offset printer, must have metal engravings to mount with the type. In a manner of speaking, offset printing handles type like pictures and prints from the image; letterpress printing handles pictures like type and prints from the raised surface. The photo (9-7) shows the raised surface of a rubber stamp, which corresponds to that of type or an engraving.

Because engravings are more expensive than art printed by offset, the use of a great deal of art or of designs that mix type and art are uneconomical. The

9-7. Letterpress printing is clearly exemplified by the raised printing surface of this rubber stamp. It reads upside down but from left to right, which is how the type compositor sets type by hand. Offset printing, in comparison, prints from a flat surface. The ink is repelled from the nonprinting surface by water and attracted to the image area by oil, based on the principle that oil and water do not mix.

9-8. Silkscreen printing holds the image on a fine screen, usually made of aluminum rather than silk, with the image area open to allow the ink or paint to pass through onto the printing surface beneath.

user should limit the size and amount of art for letterpress printing to hold down costs. This method of printing should be seen in terms of the advantages that it offers for typesetting, the convenience that it offers in revising listings set in type, and the convenience of one-stop shopping in which the typographer supplies the design, with little or no use of pictures as design elements.

Intaglio printing is designed primarily for extensive quantities and for a greater rather than a lesser use of pictures. Like offset printing, it does not discriminate between type and pictures, but, unlike offset printing, a very expensive engraved roller is used. The expense involved with intaglio printing is such that its use should not be contemplated for quantities under one hundred thousand, with cost efficiency often being achieved only with quantities of a million or more. The printing element can stand up to such a long run without wearing out. This means that the process tends to be used for extensive mailings or for large quantities of catalogs and brochures.

If such an investment for printing is considered, professionals would undoubtedly be used for all phases of the work, including design and art preparation. Art preparation is very similar to that for offset in the use of paste-up. The major difference is that any kind of art can be included with the type,

and for this reason the paste-up is sometimes done larger than actual size.

Silkscreen job printing represents the other end of the quantity scale in that it is sometimes used for as few as twenty impressions. It is done with paint rather than with ink. The photo (9-8) shows the frame for the screen hinged above the printing board, which locates the position of the surface to be printed. The ink or paint is forced with a squeegee through openings in the screen corresponding to the image to be printed. The paint provides the outstanding feature of the silkscreen process, because it can stick to a variety of surfaces such as glass or metal. This makes silkscreen printing suitable for signs or posters that will be exposed to the elements.

The mesh openings that allow the paint to reach the surface to be printed require the use of solid line art. The photographic process of making the printing screen creates fine edges so that, if a very fine screen is used, fairly small type can be printed cleanly but tonal effects are difficult to achieve. The user can avoid these problems if he uses only line art. With the use of line art and the need for a limited number of reproductions silkscreen is sometimes an economical printing method. Again, the art can be presented as a complete paste-up.

Letterpress printing is the only method in which makeup by the typographer can be economically substituted for paste-up. This is an economy measure only with the use of as little art as possible. With more extensive artwork a paste-up can again be prepared and an engraving made of everything to be printed including the type, but the cost advantage would be lost and offset printing would on balance be cheaper. The increasing use of art indicates another reason why offset printing is growing in popularity. Silkscreen and intaglio printing have special uses and advantages.

There are other special printing techniques in addition to the four methods discussed here, which are those most frequently used by the originator of art. Many technical refinements have not been presented here, but the user has the benefit of expert advice in any event. Packaging, display, and advertising specialties are best handled by professionals because they involve production considerations in addition to design considerations, and many subtleties of technique enter into production design, which are too complex for any but the specialist to work with. These areas would be handled as one handles other specialist fields such as film processing.

Film and television

Film and TV are combined in this discussion not because they are identical in technique but because the handling of art is so similar. Film can be used on television. It is important to realize, however, that videotape is an electronic recording of the cathode-ray-tube image, and the technology of this form of image recording is different from that of film images. The user, however, may present picture images for television as film, and the originator can work with film for television.

Film offers the greatest fidelity of image recording; motion-picture film is preferred to videotape for this reason. Because of the considerable expense involved in motion-picture production, film processing, and extensive TV exposure, production is usually handled by specialists and experts. In fact, motion-picture production is the most expensive of all picture uses. Super-8 and 16mm film can be used instead of the standard 35mm film to reduce costs, but the latter yields the best quality and is standard for many applications or for greatly enlarged projection.

Because of the cost factor 35mm slides are often preferred to motion-picture film for industrial applications, and audiovisuals have become very popular. Audiovisuals synchronize a sound track with automatically changed slides. The effect is somewhat similar to a motion picture, with the obvious exception that motion cannot be shown. The effect of motion can be created, however, by a series of stop-action frames. Relative to print communication, slides expand the use of illustration. Slides and audiovisual presentations have many applications for sales and industry, and the equipment is inexpensive in comparison to motion pictures.

Motion pictures, slides, and audiovisuals bring pictures into a sequential perspective. The originator must plan for the sequence and continuity of the presentation. The effect to be hoped for with use of pictures in sequence, as with the photomontage, is that the total communication is greater than the sum of the parts, because the relationship between the parts is understood. This incorporates a continuity point of view into the use of the single picture.

To develop continuity, the originator uses a storyboard technique, developed with animation, in which picture and script are placed together and action and camera movement are also described. The time-frame continuity differs from the use of a single illustration, and this factor probably accounts for the popularity of slide presentation. To be fair, the designer's work with stationary graphics does consider continuity and utilize design to direct eye movement to the desired communication: the pictures don't change but the eye moves so that the attention of the viewer changes. Picture movement, whether with motion-picture film or a slide sequence, provides the attention change for the viewer, and the use of a storyboard is a way to plan for this continuity of change.

The photo (9-10) shows a preprinted pad with a picture window proportional to a TV screen and copy space below the picture. The individual picture-frame and copy-box sheets are perforated so that they can be separated for sequence revision. Index cards or separate sheets of paper can also be used. It is sometimes convenient to mount and sequence a great number of pictures on a bulletin board. This helps the originator develop the presentation by making everything visible at the same time. The storyboard illustrates the interaction of picture and language for communication.

The originator need not be an artist to use a storyboard: the picture can be described on the card in words for the sake of planning. Even a simple slide show benefits from storyboard development, and careful planning is essential to an interesting presentation. The originator is also advised to plan and to schedule time for production and processing.

Slides are easy to obtain through normal processing channels, as is the equipment to project them. Most of us are familiar with slides, projectors, and slide presentations. Slides can be made of artwork as well as photography, and titles, diagrams, and charts can be photocopied for presentation. The user is advised not to use line-negative slides with clear areas that produce light flare but rather to substitute

background tone or color to control the light. Some cameras may need closeup attachments to photograph artwork smaller than 20 x 16 inches. The film should mount into the standard 2-x-2-inch frame used by most projectors.

Slides are held on screen for varying lengths of time during a presentation, according to their nature and appeal. No one seems to agree on the optimum length of time, but everyone agrees that it is a mistake to leave a slide on for too long. The time might vary from fifteen seconds for titles to a full minute for a diagram or chart that takes time to understand. It is sometimes desirable to duplicate a complicated slide in a later sequence.

The use of the audiovisual automates the presentation and allows the presenter time to deal with the new situation and with other requirements. The automation relieves the presenter from the need to change slides and to deal with considerations that might require two people. For longer or duplicate presentations filmstrips can be used rather than slides. Filmstrips cost less to process, make a smaller package for mailing, and maintain the picture order. The audiovisual filmstrip is also useful for repeated presentations.

Overhead projection allows the speaker to face the audience (9-11). The speaker can also permit more light in the room and use a pointer on the slide. The slides can be made economically and easily. The use of a pointer and the smaller-size viewing audience of overhead projection as compared to slide projection appear to invite more audience participation and discussion. The difficulties lie in the requirement for very exact projection, so as not to distort the picture image, and in the relative unavailability of overhead projectors. The overhead projector tends to be used as a classroom installation, not as a lightweight portable unit, although one or two are on the market.

The size of the overhead-projector slide permits easy reading and handling. The speaker can manipulate the slide and even draw or write on it. The slide is quickly made from the original at the same size with Thermofax or diazotype foil. For some ap-

9-9. This television antenna was one of the first used for public broadcasting during the forties.

plications this is convenient, but the large size is expensive if full-color or continuous-tone negatives are used. Forty or fifty overhead-projection slides also make a hefty package.

Opaque projection is the ultimate in convenience in that any graphic image can be projected without preparation. Art panels, note sheets, pages from books, photocopies, and other materials that fit the projection space can be projected. The difficulty lies in the projection. Because light diminishes by the square of the distance, projection requires an intense light and a semidark surface to be seen. The heat from this light limits viewing time and even requires some paper be mounted to prevent curling.

Slides and overhead projection pass light through the image and focus it with a lens. Overhead projection introduces a mirror, which reduces the intensity of the projected image. Opaque projection reflects light from the subject through the lens and off the mirror to the projection surface for viewing. It is like using a photoprint rather than a photographic negative for projection.

Copies of the presentation material can be supplied to the audience. Overhead and opaque projection are particularly good in this regard, and the material seen on screen can be copied at the same size from the overhead-projection slide or the original art. Slides, however, must be enlarged and printed by the photoprinting process. With quantity the photoprinting process can be automated, which reduces the cost for an enlarged photoprint to a small percentage of its unit cost when done as handwork. The photo (9-12) shows the print strip and the automated-printing machine. A glossy photograph makes an impressive presentation compared to the usual copier output and can cost only slightly more.

Titles and artwork can be used with slides, overhead projection, and opaque projection. The better the art, of course, the more interesting the presentation. With the use of transfer type titles can be made by the originator, since no drawing skill is required—only the ability to space the lettering. Slide art is done in sizes from 9 x 6 inches to 20 x 16 inches. Flip charts can also be turned into slides by photocopying. Animation is done on a standard 15½-x-12½-inch sheet—a convenient size—for

9-10. Preprinted pads with the proportions of a TV screen and a box for dialogue and camera moves assist in planning a storyboard. This example deals with a commercial for a contractor. The sections tear along perforated lines for easy sequence revision.

photographing onto motion-picture film.

Because audiovisuals are becoming so popular, specialists in film and slide art for presentation are also appearing in response to the need for this service. A number of techniques can be utilized, some with film, some with materials specifically made for slide art, some with transfer sheets and color sheets, and with a conventional opaque graphic surface, which is photographed.

Different art materials are used for an opaque surface and for slide projection, in which light must pass through the image. Materials used on an overhead-projection slide must let light pass through in order to obtain the most brilliant projected image. Art for slides can be done as an opaque image, because it must be photographed to be made into a slide. Halftone art is easier to use with slides than with overhead projection for this reason, because it must be handled as film. The user of projection is advised to be careful with type sizes; they must be

9-11. This drawing shows how overhead projection is conducive to group discussions and seminars. Audiovisuals are more common, however, because of the availability and efficiency of the equipment.

large enough to be easily read at the maximum viewing distance.

Perhaps the most conventional presentational tool is the flip chart. A flip chart is a series of large drawings that are hinged so that they can be flipped over as the talk proceeds. The drawings can also be prepared as separate cards. Flip charts and flip cards make better visuals than blackboard drawings. The audience size is limited to the distance from which the charts can be read. Because these charts must be relatively large as compared to slides, they are the bulkiest form of presentation and certainly the most difficult to travel with. In spite of their sketchy artwork flip charts can be more expensive to produce than any other form of presentation. This is because of their size and because the art must have a finished look if it is to be presented directly to the audience. Other techniques used to produce slides allow the art to be converted into the presentation element through photography or copying, which excludes the pieces and pasted elements used to assemble artwork for a slide.

It may seem strange, but the do-it-yourself visual aid can end up costing more than professional work if you proportion the costs according to the time spent in producing it. This factor may account in part for the popularity of the audiovisual, since it is more likely that it will be produced professionally. The overhead-projection slide compares unfavorably to the audiovisual slide for this reason, because it is too tempting to just type up some information and make a slide of it. On the other hand, the audiovisual is less expensive than either motion-picture film or flip charts and cards, which require a more finished art technique.

While you won't see them on national television because the cost for the time mandates a better visual presentation, flip charts are still sometimes used as a visual aid for some local television commercials, in which the cost for time is competitive with publication advertising. Because television is a visual medium, it demands a visual aid. With the proper equipment slides can be used as a visual aid for a local commercial. If the station has two cameras, the slide can be superimposed on the video picture electronically, combining the two pictures. The diagram (9-13) illustrates the use of two cameras. Typographic material on one camera can be superimposed over the picture on another camera. Slides can also be used for rear projection, providing a background of the slide image for the subject on camera. The use of these techniques can bring the viewer into the picture rather than maintaining a stationary audience view. The material used for the flip chart or the placard can be projected behind the announcer.

The most common use of the superimposed picture is to reverse the black type image, the written message, out of the picture on camera (9-14). The most common use of rear projection is to provide a background for the announcer or speaker. Both can move in the sense that written material can be scrolled in front of the supercamera, as is so commonly done with credits; the rear projection can be taken in a tighter shot and the camera panned over the picture.

With only one camera and facilities for rear projection the slide can be changed behind the announcer on camera, and a written message can be handled

9-12. The strip is an example of the use of mechanized printing for quantity reproduction of the film print. Mechanization sharply reduces the cost for a large number of photoprints. The illustration is used by courtesy of PIC.

as rear projection. This allows for camera movement between the projection and the announcer, as a viewer would follow a slide presentation.

The use of the audiovisual is similar in a way to the use of television. It is an improvement to the extent that the camera viewpoint coincides with the movement of the viewer's interest and that the subject of interest is shown in closeup. The camera becomes a subjective guide, moving as one's visual interest moves. For communication this is the movie formula of long shot to orient the viewer, intermediate shot to focus attention, and closeup shot to show action. Because sound is incorporated with visual impression and movement, much sensory information is communicated simultaneously. That all this is assimilated as idea or concept is useful to communication.

Television is visual communication, even if it is also auditory communication. It appears that we are more oriented to the visual than to the auditory for whatever reason: sayings such as "I'll believe it when I see it" emphasize the visual. Television trains this faculty still further. Is it any wonder that pictures are useful as a medium for communication?

We ought to think in terms of the picture and communicate with the vision of the poet. With the means to make pictures part of our graphic communication through the use of reprographics, print, and film we should say it with pictures.

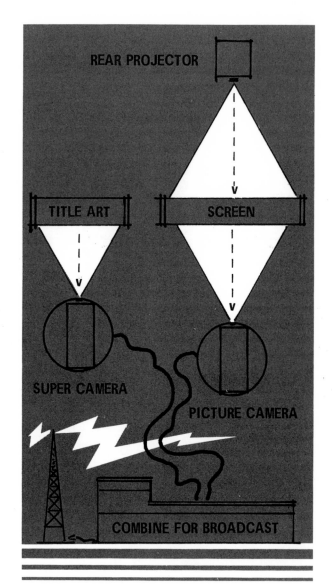

9-13. Provided that the equipment is available, the diagram above shows that two cameras are an improvement upon flip cards for local-TV-station commercials.

9-14. The series of illustrations at right shows how the separate elements are combined electronically to make a composite picture. The illustration art and the heading are produced separately.

INDEX